What's Wrong with Eating People?

Cave is not just a very gifted philosopher, he's also clear, captivating and funny too.

Stephen Law, Author of The Philosophy Gym

Your personal philosophy trainer. The puzzles offer you a heady work out, leaving you fitter to fight your own intellectual corner.

Mark Vernon, Author of 42: Deep Thought on Life, the Universe and Everything

Delightfully written and fun to read. Witty and eloquent and the puzzles are explored throughout with both common sense and wisdom.

Anthony Ellis, Professor of Philosophy, Virginia Commonwealth University

Energetic, highly entertaining, and delightfully thought-provoking.

A. W. Moore, Professor of Philosophy, University of Oxford

Provocative and lively. Few would fail to be stimulated by these puzzles.

Oliver Leaman, Professor of Philosophy, University of Kentucky

About the Author

Writer and broadcaster Peter Cave teaches philosophy for The Open University and City University London. Author of the bestselling *Can A Robot be Human?*, he chairs the Humanist Philosophers' Group and is often in debate, talking about paradoxes, and arguing for good reasoning, especially in ethical, political, and religious life. He frequently contributes to philosophy journals and magazines, from the academic to the popular, lectures abroad, and has introduced BBC radio listeners to a paradoxical fair of fun. Philosophy and reflection, he feels, are often helped when enlivened with tales, images, and a few touches of humour.

What's Wrong with Eating People?

33 More Perplexing Philosophy Puzzles

Peter Cave

ONEWORLD
OXFORD

A Oneworld Paperback Original

Published by Oneworld Publications 2008
Reprinted 2008

Copyright © Peter Cave 2008

ISBN 978–1–85168–620–9

Typeset by Jayvee, Trivandrum, India
Illustrations © www.fordcartoon.com
Cover design by James Nunn
Printed and bound in Great Britain by CPI Cox & Wyman

Oneworld Publications
185 Banbury Road
Oxford OX2 7AR
England
www.oneworld-publications.com

For:

those who wonder —
and those who do not —
and Ardon Lyon (again)

CONTENTS

PREFACE

Time would have passed anyway.

There is nothing that you need to know to enjoy this book. Well, I exaggerate – but only a little. Are you able to read English? – an interesting question. After all, even though we have probably never met, you know and I know that the answer is 'yes'. That hurdle is already jumped; you have read this far. There are also the hurdles of being able and willing to think. These too are jumped; reading requires both – and you are still reading … so far.

Reading is an amazing activity. Look at any sentence in a language that you know. It is exceedingly difficult to see it solely as a set of printed shapes. You cannot help but see the shapes as words; you cannot help but see through to some meaning. Yet whatever is this thing called 'meaning'? Already we are beginning to philosophize – and when, in our daily lives, we praise people, fall in love or wonder what it is rational to do, lurking within are philosophical positions about how free people are, about desires, choices, and reasoning.

Virtually every discussion, argument, reflection we have – be it in the pub, newspaper or bath – embodies some philosophical assumptions and questions. Here, I bring some to light, sometimes playfully, sometimes provocatively, be it through phantasies, dialogues or straight reports. Of course, 'enjoyment' in dipping may not be the right expression; but I am sure that the discussions are sufficiently intriguing for you to muse upon further and probably with others. I am sure because, as humans, we possess a reflective and social curiosity. And that curiosity is not just a way of passing the time. Indeed, as has been said, time would have passed anyway. The curiosity is about human life and our understanding of the world – including, for that matter, our understanding of time.

The puzzles, paradoxes, and perplexities presented here range across the gamut of human life, and – despite the subtitle – far exceed thirty-three. Some directly concern rationality and reasoning, logic and language; but many spread way beyond, into ethics, the arts, mind, and law – into, indeed, whether eating people is wrong. They transport us from how great God may be to whether women and men are equal; from why we should save endangered species to muddles in reasoning – to what is this thing called 'love'?

Philosophy opens eyes; philosophy opens 'I's

Simply by virtue of belonging to a community of speakers, we possess materials for philosophizing. There need be no special demands for mathematical ability, erudite historical knowledge or scientific investigations – just our everyday experiences. In a way, philosophy is neither as difficult as Sudoku nor as annoyingly cryptic as some crosswords. Yet, in another way, philosophy presents hugely greater challenges and rewards – not least because we may never be sure when we have finished. The puzzles may persist; perhaps some are inescapable. Of course, philosophy is no mere matter of fun; philosophy grapples with basic understandings and misunderstandings.

Philosophy knows no bounds. Philosophers will puzzle about anything. They will puzzle – yet also aim to clarify. Well, that is how many philosophers see their task. This may challenge some recent 'postmodernists' who often appear to value obscurity. I have in mind the excesses of Derrida, Irigaray, and Kristeva – but perhaps the problem is mine, in failing to comprehend. Of course, the puzzles in this book give rise to many perplexities; but I hope they do not result from the writing's obscurity. The perplexities are present at a much deeper level – when we are reflecting on the world, humanity, and, yes, reflecting on language and reflecting on reflecting.

Philosophy opens eyes. Seneca of ancient Rome commented how things of daily occurrence, even when most worthy of amazement and admiration, pass us by unnoticed. We may be likened, on occasions, to sleepwalkers, successfully finding our way about, yet unaware of what we are doing. Philosophy opens our eyes indeed. Philosophy, it has been suggested, opens our eyes to what we already know – itself a paradoxical thought.

Philosophy also opens 'I's. Once in worldly reflection, we may soon be wondering about ourselves – or, better, our and others' *selves*. We use the word 'I' thousands of times each day, yet quite what is the self, or the selves, of which we speak? What makes my self a different self from yours? – puzzles found in Chapters 18 and 6, *The brain* and *'Hi, I'm Sir Isaac Newton – don't mention the apples'*.

Brain food – *or* philosophy through puzzles

Philosophy can generate light – unlike treadmills at gyms. Although ungymed myself, I recognize that exercising the body is popular and valuable. However, we also need some exercising of the mind. Philosophy provides the opportunity – and provides the opportunity about matters that matter. Philosophy does not just help to keep our minds active and alert; it involves us, as said, in some of humanity's deepest questions. It may even generate some welcome humility: must all puzzles have solutions?

The term 'paradox' is sometimes confined to apparent contradictions within logic and mathematics. Often, though, philosophers use 'paradox' more widely – as I do here – where the words 'paradoxes', 'puzzles', and 'perplexities' are more or less interchangeable. In the philosophical puzzles here – the paradoxes, the perplexities – we often start off with some comments, our beliefs or principles, which appear obviously true. These are the premisses. We do some reasoning; and so we expect to reach conclusions that we should accept. Paradox arises because the reached conclusions hit us as manifestly false, unacceptable or undesirable. In some way they contradict our starting beliefs. Something must have gone wrong with the reasoning – or maybe our starting points are mistaken. The perplexity resides in locating the mistakes.

Some philosophical puzzles puzzle because we are unsure how far to take, or where to take, our principles or everyday beliefs. We realize that if we go so far, then we hit some crazy stances, stances that contradict other beliefs – but how can we stop ourselves from hitting such cases?

Contradictions are ...? Oops – does that suggest a need to learn some new concepts? Not at all. Early on, I wrote of reading. In reading, we show awareness of contradictions and related concepts. Our grasp is part of our everyday use of language – even though we may lack formal definitions.

You come home and find two notes left by your partner. One says, 'Wait in for me,' the other says, 'Don't wait in for me.' What do you do? These are contradictory instructions – so, quite reasonably, you are baffled. Hence, we need to avoid contradictions – to avoid being *contra* in speech or diction. This avoidance applies beyond instructions. Your friend tells you, 'It will rain today,' and then adds 'It won't rain today.' Again, you are baffled – baffled concerning what she believes and what you should do umbrella-wise. Because we seek understanding we may try to explain away the contradictions: maybe the notes show a mind change; maybe the speaker of rain speaks of different places.

Suppose your friends hold that people ought not to harm others, but then it turns out that they often fight and hurt each other – well, we should feel some contradiction has arisen. Again, we may search for consistency. Perhaps the principle has exceptions when it comes to self-defence or consent: perhaps the fighting is consensual boxing. Many ethical puzzles, though, rarely have such simple resolutions: see Chapter 30, *If this be judging...*

Talking the sun down – and
Can a Robot be Human?

This book is eminently dippable. It is also structured to flit you, to and fro, between different topics, if read straight through. If, instead, you follow the arrows at each chapter's end, then you will initially stay with certain themes, but be led to others.

This book can, of course, be read totally separately from my first collection of thirty-three puzzles, *Can a Robot be*

Human? Which puzzles appeared in which book was pretty arbitrary. 'All things conspire' is an ancient saw – and certainly in philosophy, one puzzle leads to another. This applies within this book as well as between the two books. Hence, I have included an appendix of main puzzle areas, referring to both books – for if a puzzle particularly intrigues here, you may want to pursue related ones in *Robot*.

Philosophy is usually seen as a social pursuit – people in dialogue, with some cut and some thrust – so, let me recommend that you raise these questions at home, at college, at work; in the pub, over dinner, down at the football, or when lolling on holiday hammocks. And then see how reflections and puzzlements blossom forth. You will probably find you can talk the sun down – and up again.

Wittgenstein, arguably the twentieth century's greatest philosopher, suggested that, when two philosophers meet, their greeting should be 'Take your time'. Returning us to the preface's motto, my recommended approach to reading and thinking about these matters is, indeed, Wittgenstein's.

Take your time.

ACKNOWLEDGEMENTS

As with *Can a Robot be Human?* I am indebted to many col-
leagues and students, over the years, at The Open University
and City University London. Instead of re-naming names
from *Robot*, let me thank all who have helped me as before. I
also thank again the editors of *Philosophy Now*, *The Philosophers'*
Magazine, and *Think*, for publishing my light articles, two or
three having been adapted here.

Particular useful comments derive from Sir David
Blatherwick, Laurence Goldstein, Martin Holt, Julian
Mayers, Anthony Savile, Raymond Tallis, and Jerry Valberg. I
thank them all – and apologize to those I have forgotten.
Arnold Zuboff kindly spent much time failing to guide me
along truth's path concerning Sleeping Beauty.

Much of the writing took place in the British Library;
and my thanks go to its helpful staff. For additional practical
help, I thank Malcolm Fleming and Debra Harris – and, for

supporting my labours indirectly, Phil Smith, Sally Mitchell, and Tony Seaton. Many thanks, too, to Juliet Mabey, Mike Harpley, Kate Smith, and all at Oneworld. As ever, for many valuable aiding ways, my special gratitude goes to Angela Joy Harvey.

The philosopher who has suffered most in this enterprise is Ardon Lyon – from whom I continue to learn much. He has read all the material at draft stages, with his usual good humour, meticulous attention, astonished expressions, and outrageous laughs. I cannot help but add that he is not responsible. Did I mean that?

Peter Cave

1

ON THINKING TOO MUCH:
HOW NOT TO WIN A PRINCESS'S HAND

Cast ourselves into a kingdom, a kingdom ruled by the king and queen, a kingdom with jesters, princes, and princesses, with dragons, dreams, and damsels in distress. In our kingdom, there is a beautiful princess, the king and queen's daughter; yet there is stalemate: which young man should gain the princess's hand? The king wants his daughter to marry Prince Clever, who is indeed clever, though neither exactly handsome nor strong nor possessing a prince's charm. The queen backs a rival, Prince Not So Clever, who is assuredly not so clever, yet is handsome, manly, and charming. Both young men are enchanted by the princess. And the princess's love concerning the young men? Well, she wisely lets it be known she could love either; she does not want to make enemies of her father or mother. Such is love in those days – and such is parental authority.

'We must set the suitors a task,' declares the queen, 'to see who displays the greatest devotion to our daughter.'

'What a good idea,' agrees the king. 'Let it be a mathematical puzzle and one that …'

'Of course not,' insists the queen, knowing Prince Not So Clever would fail any such test. 'They must slay a dragon. The first suitor to return with a dragon suitably slain shall have our daughter's hand.'

Now, that is not as impossible a task as it may sound; this is a kingdom with convenient dragons ready to be slain. Our princes, though, lack eagerness toward the proposal – after all, dragon-slaying is hard work and can be quite a heated affair – but, if it has to be done, it would be worth the effort for the princess's hand. The king is very unhappy at the proposal; his preferred candidate would be highly unlikely to win.

The king and queen argue until the princess pipes up. 'Let it be that one of the men needs *only* to *intend* to slay a dragon, while the other must actually slay a dragon.' At this, Prince Clever quickly bags the 'intention only' option, thinking that would obviously be so much easier than all the messy effort of slaying. Prince Not So Clever sighs, accepting that his slow-wittedness means that he will have to do the slaying.

'This is pointless and silly,' thunders the queen, then muttering, 'Prince Not So Clever is bound to lose – *intending*, which is all Prince Clever has to do, is so much easier than actually doing.' Yet the princess kicks her, politely of course, silencing her – such is daughterly authority in those days.

And so, it is decided that the winner of the princess's hand will be the one who completes his task first, be it the intending only, sincerely of course, or the actual slaying, starting at sunrise tomorrow. Before readers ask, the king and queen have a court mind-reader who can easily read minds for sincere intentions. If this worries readers, we pop into the kingdom future brain scanners that readily detect psychological states such as intentions. Now, the question is:

Who is more likely to win the princess's hand?

The puzzle centres on rationality and affects our everyday lives. In our question, we have added the caveat of 'more likely' as protection from readers who rightly note that we have said nothing about how strong the local dragons are, exactly how clever the suitors are, whether they remember the task next morning, and so on. Assuming all is straightforward, other than the tale's oddness, the answer, as readers may have guessed, is that Prince Not So Clever wins. He gets on with his task, slays the dragon, and marries the princess. What goes wrong for Prince Clever?

Prince Clever was, of course, eager to accept the condition whereby merely intending was sufficient to win the princess's hand. As the queen thought, merely intending to do something seems so much easier than actually doing. Indeed, we may well sincerely intend to perform feats, yet fail. Prince Clever mused upon this point.

'I need only to intend to slay a dragon,' he reflected. 'The actual slaying is hard work; so it would be silly to do any slaying, once that, at sunrise, I have already intended to slay … Ah, but that means that I would not be sincerely intending to slay after all – if I know that I won't then bother to slay.'

Prince Clever thought more. 'Ah well, I'd better slay the dragon after all,' he reflected miserably, but then hesitated. 'Hold on, that would be crazy, for I don't need to do that, once I have had my sincere sunrise intention to slay. Yet as I am aware of that, once again I should have failed to have formed the required sincere intention. Okay, I had better go and slay – but hold on …'

And so Prince Clever's reasoning looped round and round – and as the sun rose he still found himself unable to form a sincere intention. Whenever he said 'I intend', trying to mean it, his reason reminded him that he would not need to do what he intended – and he would have good reason not to do it, when the time came. Of course, Prince Not So Clever lacked all such quandaries; he went out and slew the dragon. Mind you, it was a little dragon.

And so it was that Prince Not So Clever married the princess. The princess pretended surprise, while within she smiled wisely. Such was princesses' wisdom in those days.

*　　　*　　　*

Had the mere 'intention' requirement also been given to Prince Not So Clever, he would still have won. Being not so clever, he would not have become enmeshed in the clever reasoning of Prince Clever. The puzzle arises because, at times, it is rational to commit ourselves to doing something that, later on, it will be irrational to do. When we reflect on this, we see how rationally we should lose the motivation to do the irrational, once that 'later on' comes, thus undermining our commitment now to performing the task in question.

Had Prince Clever been cleverer, maybe he could have persuaded himself that the requirement was that he really did have to slay the dragon rather than merely intend to slay: he would have been better off having that false belief. Or perhaps he could have committed himself to behaving irrationally in the future.

The general puzzle here concerns binding ourselves over the future. Prince Clever needed to bind himself to carrying out his intention, blocking his ears from reason's nagging little voice, reminding him that he would not need to do the slaying, if only he could intend to slay. In more everyday scenarios, things are a little different. Reason may tell us that we should arrange circumstances to prevent ourselves from yielding to future temptations; yet paradoxically we may know that, when faced with those temptations, we shall see things differently and fully favour succumbing.

There is the ancient Greek tale according to which Odysseus knew that, unrestrained, he would yield to the sirens when he heard their melodious and beguiling song. Hence, he told his sailors to bind him to the mast and stop their ears with beeswax, ensuring that they would not hear his orders to be released, when tempted by the song. Thus it was that, paradoxically, Odysseus intentionally prevented himself from doing what he would later want to do.

These days we rarely encounter sirens seeking to sing us to the grave. We may, though, somewhat more prosaically, be aware that, as the evening draws on, we are likely to eat too many chocolates or drink too much wine; so we deliberately avoid buying these goods of delight on the way home. Yet we know that we shall soon be regretting that earlier decision.

Did our past selves, so to speak, have a right to bind us to this sober, chocolate-less evening?

And as we puzzle that question, we may more urgently puzzle whether the local supermarket is still open — or whether, hold on … Isn't there some whisky tucked away upstairs?

3. A PILL FOR EVERYTHING?

17. GOD, CHOCOLATE, AND NEWCOMB: TAKE THE BOX?

20. HOW TO GAIN WHATEVER YOU WANT

6. 'HI, I'M SIR ISAAC NEWTON – DON'T MENTION THE APPLES'

2

ON THE RUN: ALL'S FAIR WITH BEARS?

Here are two explorers. Let them be Penelope Pessimist and Ophelia Optimist. They are exploring some mountainous regions, when they become suddenly aware of a bear in the distance, a bear big and hungry and intent upon feeding – feeding upon them. The bear heads in their direction, picking up speed, anticipating a tasty explorer breakfast.

'We'd better run for it,' urges Ophelia Optimist.

'What's the point?' sighs Penelope Pessimist in despair at the bear. 'There's no way we can outrun a bear.'

'No need to do that,' smirks Ophelia Optimist. 'No need for *us* to outrun the bear – just for *me* to outrun *you*.' And with that, she was off.

*　　*　　*

What are we morally allowed to do to save our lives? Assuming the bear needs to breakfast on only one, either

could sacrifice herself. But does morality demand such self-sacrifice? And who should do the sacrificing? Before readers ask, let us assume that both women know that they cannot overpower the bear. Running is the only answer. In such circumstances, looking after oneself seems, at the very least, morally permissible.

Let us delete Ophelia's smirk. Both explorers recognize the tragedy of their plight. They recognize that it would be beyond the call of morality for Ophelia to have to sacrifice herself – or, indeed, for Penelope to do so. They both race away from the bear, not knowing who is faster or more skilled at twists and turns; they are letting fortune determine which one escapes – and which one dies.

The outcome, though, could be certain. They may know that Ophelia is the faster runner and will escape; so Penelope will provide the bear's breakfast. If so, then Ophelia is letting the weaker, Penelope, go to the wall – more accurately, to the bear's digestion. Yet that is no good reason for Ophelia to sacrifice herself. After all, were she to make such a sacrifice, we could wonder why Penelope ought not to be sacrificing herself instead. And what value exists in their both yielding to the bear? They are not lovers who cannot live without each other.

Let us modify the tale: the only way one can be sure of escape is by tripping up the other. We probably think that doing that would be morally wrong. Maybe it is unfair; it is unfair for one woman deliberately to interfere with the other. Yet how is it fair in the first place that one woman runs faster than the other?

Is it morally permissible for you to save your life, if an innocent individual's death results?

We swim in murky waters here. Let us focus. Consider only cases in which the life of solely one innocent person is lost through saving your own life. To avoid complexities of families, lifespan, and so on, we assume that the individuals involved have similar responsibilities and potential for happiness and contributions to society.

Here are some different scenarios to test what we sense is permissible. Suppose that Ophelia and Penelope are in a queue, Ophelia at the front. A crazed individual is facing the queue, firing a revolver. Ophelia ducks to avoid being shot; as a result, the bullet kills Penelope. Ophelia, in defending herself, helps to bring about Penelope's death. Yet even if she foresees that Penelope will be shot – perhaps Ophelia lacks time to warn her – Ophelia does not intend Penelope's death. Her death is not the means whereby Ophelia saves herself. Had everyone in the queue ducked, maybe no one would have been killed. Penelope was an innocent and unlucky bystander.

Contrast the above with a different 'queue' example where Ophelia, to avoid being shot, pushes Penelope in front of her. Here, Ophelia is using Penelope as a shield – without informed consent. Surely, Ophelia is not morally permitted to do that. This suggests that an important, morally relevant feature is whether a person is being endangered through being used as a means of defence. We see this in another contrast:

A run-away tram hurtles towards you. You are trapped on the tracks, but you have a wireless points' control, so you are able to divert the tram onto a siding, thus saving yourself. Unfortunately, you know that there is a worker lying unconscious on the siding's tracks. By diverting, you save your life, yet bring about the worker's death. That may or may not be morally permissible, but it certainly is not as bad as what you do in the next scenario.

Once again, the run-away tram is hurtling towards you. The only means of saving your life is by firing a rubber bullet at a passer-by near the track. The passer-by, stunned, falls onto the track and is killed by the tram, bringing it to a halt. Thus, you are saved, saved by using the passer-by as a shield. The passer-by's death is the *means* whereby you are saved, unlike the worker's death.

When we use someone as a shield, we are transferring our misfortune to someone else who is required to suffer. There are, then, two morally relevant factors.

One factor concerns the misfortune transferred and its significance for the recipient. If the only way to save my life is by causing an innocent person 'as a shield' to have her nail varnish tarnished – well, that is morally acceptable; and if the shield protests, then she displays selfishness, lacking a sense of proportion. If I grab the fine silk scarf from a gentleman, the scarf needed to stem arterial blood flowing from my thigh, I have doubtless invaded his property; but saving a life at the cost of a silk scarf is a good deal, even if he complains about my violation of his property rights.

The second factor concerns the transference itself. In the shield examples it is deliberate and required. In the other examples, the life would be saved, even if no misfortunes were to occur to others. We may, though, question this distinction's relevance, if we know the misfortunes will in fact occur. You have a right to defend yourself from the tram by diverting it; but if you foresee that the worker's death will result, are you not behaving cruelly in passing that misfortune buck onto him? Of course, morally things are different, if you know that he is conscious and could leap free to safety, with or without his nail varnish tarnished. However, in the case set out, you are surely not morally justified in passing the deadly tram onto him. The unconscious worker is, so to speak, an innocent threat to you – a threat in that his presence morally prevents you from doing what would otherwise be permissible to save your life, namely, diverting the tram.

*   *   *

Returning to the bear, where does this leave the morality, or otherwise, of Ophelia taking to her heels, knowing that Penelope is likely to be eaten? After all, Penelope does need to be caught and feasted upon, to ensure that the bear does not continue to chase Ophelia. It may appear as if Ophelia is passing her misfortune onto Penelope – and hence it is as morally bad as your diverting the tram onto the unconscious worker. Yet we may feel that here 'every woman for herself' is morally acceptable.

Perhaps the relevant difference between the shield and bear examples concerns the tales' starting points. With the bear, the two explorers are in it together from the start; both are exposed to the bear's hungry eye. With the tram example, you alone are initially exposed to the danger. If you take no action, the worker is safe. If Ophelia takes no action regarding the bear, Penelope may still be exposed to the bear's dining desires. If the crazed gunman is out to shoot anyone, then again we may think that all in the queue are party to the misfortune. Suppose, though, that the gunman is specifically after Ophelia at the front of the queue. By diving down, avoiding the bullets, has she unfairly transferred a misfortune buck to others?

The worker on the track, Penelope standing behind Ophelia in the queue, Penelope being less adept at running – we may voice the mantra proclaiming the unfairness of all these conditions. Yet, of course, there is also the unfairness of Ophelia's happening to be at the queue's front, your being in the path of the runaway tram – and, spreading the net much wider, the unfairness of many being born into war, poverty, and disease, when many are not.

As with many moral matters, over what to do, it seems – well, all we can do is muddle through.

22. VEILS OF WOE: BEATS AND PEEPING TOMS TOO

12. 'WOMEN AND MEN ARE EQUAL' – REALLY?

5. MAN WITH PULLEY: WAVING OR DROWNING?

3

A PILL FOR EVERYTHING?

Consider this little dialogue.

'Madam, may I help you?'

'I doubt it. I so want that red dress, but it's way, way too expensive, way beyond my means.'

'Madam, how about the blue? It's equally attractive, yet so much cheaper – I mean, more competitively priced.'

'Mmm, I could afford the blue; but I never feel comfortable in blue – even though people always tell me how it suits me. I'm always happier with red.'

'No problem at all, madam – with the blue comes an optional pill, take the pill and you'll find you like the blue.'

'Not sure. I don't like popping pills – artificial stuff, not me.'

'Not really, madam – if I may be so bold to disagree. You would like the blue dress, if only you could overcome your discomfort with the colour. The pill is merely helping you to get what you truly want.'

'That's true, I suppose. Some people don't want to be smokers, yet cannot give up smoking, without some external assistance.'

'Exactly, madam.'

'That's all very well, but I still don't like the idea of using external help such as pills.'

'No problem at all. We can give you a pill to overcome that.'

'But that's missing the point. I'm not the sort of person who wants her system meddled with in these ways.'

'May I ask: are you satisfied being that sort of person? Wouldn't you prefer to be the sort of person who doesn't mind about these things?'

'Yes, perhaps.'

'If so, then take this other pill – it will help you to be that sort of person you would prefer to be – and look, it has a nice red colour.'

'But I can't decide what sort of person I'd rather be.'

'No problem, madam. We have a pill which will make you decide firmly one way or the other.'

'But which way is that?'

'Well, that depends which pill you take – the red or the blue, madam?'

When do I get what I truly want?

We could have added 'or the yellow, or the green, or the white' – and so on – for there are many, many ways our lives would be changed, for better or worse, by outside interferences. Yet do we have any clear idea of what counts as outside and inside? Of what counts as being truly what *I* want rather than imposed upon me? This is the puzzle at the heart of the Pill Puzzle. We tend to think of impositions as external physical obstacles or threats, yet sometimes we feel buffeted by our own desires, yearnings, and longings; we would prefer to be without them – be they sexual lusts, gluttony, or obsessive fears.

Consider smokers: they want cigarettes. Their desires may result from years of advertising combined with genetic dispositions or rebellious youth. They are smokers; yet some do not want to be smokers. They want not to have their smoking wants. There is a second-order want: a want about their first-order wants. Maybe we – friends, society, the government – should help them to become non-smokers. We could ostracize them, bar them from lighting up, but that does not directly quell their smoking desires. Maybe we could inject them with drugs that destroy the smoke-filled yearnings. What can be wrong with that, given that they do want to stop smoking?

Their freedom to smoke – the opportunity, the 'negative freedom' as it is known – is interfering with their second-order desire becoming satisfied, the desire to be non-smokers, their 'positive freedom'. We may restrict their negative free-dom – place obstacles in the way of their smoking – in order to promote their positive freedom, to be non-smokers. This is when we may quip: we are forcing them to be free – but it is not really a forcing. After all, they do explicitly own their second-order desire to be non-smokers.

That may be all well and good; but now consider smokers who seemingly lack the second-order desire to give up smok-ing. We may insist that really they do possess that second-order desire: at least, *were* they fully informed of health hazards, rationally grasping their best interests, they would be wanting to be non-smokers. This, however, is where 'forc-ing someone to be free' seems but rhetoric to justify forcing people to do what they do not want to do, even though, maybe, they ought to want to become non-smokers.

At times we do force people to behave in a certain way, in their best interests. Parents and other authorities do this with children, the mentally disturbed, and some drug addicts. But we need to be careful when we take this step: it is better to call a spade 'a spade'. These people are often being compelled to do what they really do not want to do; however, once changed as a result, they may be thankful.

*   *   *

We have spoken of first-order and second-order desires. We could dream up more orders. Some end up regarding a per-son as consisting of battling selves. A third self, so to speak, may enter the picture, adjudicating between, say, the conflicting desires of the self who wants to smoke and the self who wants to give up. We may then picture a fourth, trying to referee between the first three – and so on. That is an unhappy way to view things. Perhaps we need simply to see ourselves as often possessing conflicting desires which we reflect on, trying to decide which it is best to satisfy – though how that reflection and decision can be understood, without there being another desire thrown into the pot, remains mysterious.

Talk of second-order desires may slip us into treating them as 'higher' in the sense of 'better'; but that need not be so – and, even if the second-order are somehow more worthy, the individual may still not identify with them. A woman loves dancing and jazz, yet her extreme Protestant church tells her that such things are sinful. As a result, she develops the second-order desire not to be someone who loves dancing and jazz. Yet it is far from obvious that satisfying that second-order desire is in her best interests. She may be true to herself, if she resisted that second-order sermon-based desire. Of course, that expression 'true to herself' raises the question of which of our desires are truly ours.

There is a tendency to believe that science can solve everything. If you are unhappy about complexion and bust size, have cosmetic surgery; if addicted to gambling, pop into the addiction clinic. Surgery, pills, therapy – numerous treatments are available to give us what we want, assuming the ability to pay. Dangers arise when treatments are applied to give us what we *truly, deeply* want, whether or not we know of that want. Think historically of the many authorities that have forced people to change their behaviour 'in their best interests'. Think of authoritarian religions and political regimes that compel people to 'realize' that they do not truly want to be homosexual or atheist or promiscuous or capitalist or Protestant or Muslim … The list could go on. Protestors who would otherwise be cast into gaol – a bad enough outcome – find themselves in psychiatric units, minds, not just bodies, undergoing change and restraint.

Neither medicine nor religion nor governments – nor the moon and the stars – can ultimately tell us what we truly want. For that matter, we cannot tell what we truly want, *if*, in order to do so, we must find a 'self' – what I truly am – that has not resulted from outside causes. This is not because the search is so difficult, the self so elusive. It is because there is not a something, a self existing, unburdened by a past, uncaused by an outside.

We are layers of criss-crossing imprints and reflections; imprints from parents, schoolings, and chance encounters; reflections when planning, yearning, and remembering. We can be whirlpools of conflicting emotions and passions, of decisions and agitations, of admirations and jealousies. When the chaos is widespread and embracing, we are not in control; that is when we agonize about what we 'truly' want. Yet, once we begin to see structure, once we identify with projects and stances, we gain a sense of what we truly want, of what sort of character we truly are. To search after something more in 'truly' wanting, in 'truly' being, is to search after a chimera, an illusion, an impossibility. And, being an impossibility, it is not only impossible to have, but also not worth the having. Far better to focus on bringing order to any chaos in our lives – or, even, simply enjoying the chaos.

After all, too much order can be boring, whereas some degree of chaos can be fun.

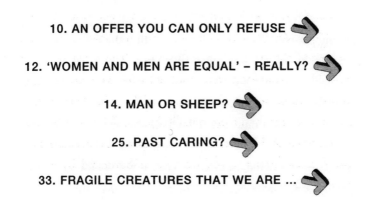

4

IN NO TIME AT ALL

Many people quite naturally accept that the future does not exist – by which they mean that future events, being in the future, are not yet existing. Similarly, it may seem obvious that the past does not exist – by which is meant that it does not exist now. It once existed, when present; but it no longer exists. Those chocolates, our tasting them and delight in them, once existed, but exist no more, being now in the past. Right now maybe you are looking forward to the future, to your next summer holiday; so, the holiday does not exist now, but it will exist. Of course, your looking forward exists; the looking forward is in the present.

All this seems obvious. The further thought, also obvious, is the conclusion that anything which exists can exist only in the present, only now. But what is the present? What is *now*?

People impressed with the above thoughts may yet slip into giving an answer by way of duration. *Now* lasts for a few minutes, or a second, or a split second – and so on. But anything suggested which has duration hits the buffers of the reflections above; well, so it would seem. If it has duration, it has parts, a beginning and end. If we are at the beginning, then the end must be in the future and hence fails to exist. If we are at the end, then the beginning must be in the past and hence fails to exist. We, here in the present, are squeezed into no time – into *no time* at all.

When we reflect on these arguments, we see the present as metaphorically going, going, gone. Nothing is left. But if neither the past nor the future exists, and if the present gets squeezed into nothing, can there be anything – just anything – that exists in time?

Can anything exist in time?

The above argument has led us to think of the present as a boundary, a boundary between past and future. Yet, if neither past nor future exists, how can a boundary exist between them? And if this supposed boundary is without duration, then quite what existence does the boundary possess – and hence quite what can possibly exist in the present? We may also wonder what happens to time itself in all of this. We seem to run out of time, for time itself seems to be squeezed out of all existence.

For many philosophers, the paradox arises because we are misled by our language of 'past, present, future', the language of tenses, with talk of what *was*, what *is*, and what *will be*. Perhaps, instead of thinking of such tensed time as basic, we should understand time in terms of events happening *before* and *after*, or *simultaneously*, with certain other events. On this latter view, if I say that the goose is now cooking in the oven, then that amounts to making the point that it is cooking simultaneously with my saying.

If time is properly captured simply by events being in the before–after series, then the events are equally real, equally exist, whether or not we describe them as being past, present, or future. A tree extended in the three spatial dimensions, with length, breadth, and height, has time as a fourth dimension; its roots are spatially below its branches and its temporal stage of being a sapling is before its temporal stage of being a mature oak. This is the tenseless view of time.

On the tenseless view, our talk in terms of tenses arises out of the fact that the different judgements we make stand in different positions in the before–after series. Time is being seen as a fourth dimension: the past, present, and future are then usually considered to be in the same boat, all existing. The future is some temporal distance away from us *now* – just as Pluto is some spatial distance away from us *here*. Future events, years away from us, exist, just as events millions of miles away from us exist. It is simply that we lack easy access to events a long way away, be they 'away' in space or in time.

Were the tenseless view of time correct, then there should be no puzzle about events existing in the present: they are as real whether they exist in the present or past or future. However, we confront different puzzles. We may wonder why it is that we cannot perceive – see, hear, smell – those events that are existing further along the before–after sequence, in either direction, in what we think of as the past and the future.

There are, of course, answers – even acceptable answers. Causes operate in one direction in the before–after series: events *before* cause events *after*, and not vice versa. Events after your reading this page, events 'in the future', cannot cause events before them. That is why, even though those future events exist, they cannot affect us now; that is why we cannot, for example, see which football team is winning next week.

What of events that occurred before your reading of this page? On the tenseless view, they too exist. And, in fact, we do perceive some of those events, events that are existing in the past. Think of the spatial distance of planets and stars. Given that light does not travel from A to B instantaneously, the changes that we see are ones that occurred at points in the time dimension well before our seeing them; they caused our seeing them. Indeed, if we think that A's causing B always takes some time, however short, then we are always experiencing things that have already happened, that are, at least a little bit, in the past.

The biggest problem with the tenseless view of time is its failure to do justice to change. The cooking goose is changing colour, changing from being raw to cooked. This is not merely a variation akin to the way in which the goose is spatially variable, with skin on the outside, bones within. Spatially, a cake may be chocolate on the outside and cream inside, but the cake is not thereby undergoing a change. Think of how different the chocolate *changing* into cream is from there simply being chocolate next to cream.

Returning to the goose, the change as it cooks seems to make essential reference to tenses: the goose was raw, but will be well done. Yet, if we are back with time understood as involving tenses, involving change, we are back with our initial puzzle.

* * *

Arguably, some of the puzzles to do with the present can be dispelled, by separating out features of time that are easily confused. Events and actions – the cooking, the handshaking, the crashing tree – take time to occur, yet they may be in the present; they are happening now. That would be impossible, were the present just a boundary or instant. Right now, you are reading this book; the present century is the twenty-first; and your present age is ... – well, complete at your discretion. What is present now is typically understood as being more than a moment. Perhaps this should lead us to accept that the present in a way includes at least portions of the past. If so, then the past, at least to some extent, and also the present certainly do exist.

That the present century is the twenty-first does not, of course, imply that we are experiencing the present century now from beginning to end in one go. What we experience as *now* is of very short duration, but still has duration. What we experience as now also differs from the period that we are able to keep before the forefront of our mind. This latter period is often known as the 'specious present', though characterizations of the specious present vary.

We can hold before our minds durations, the specious presents, that are longer than what we experience as now. Yet the 'now' durations that we experience should still be distinguished from any durationless boundaries. These distinctions, though, do not save us from bafflements about time. We now meet bafflements about the relationship between the specious present, the experienced present, and any durationless boundary.

One way of feeling the power of puzzling time, and how time strikes us, is to wonder quite what is going on when we listen to a piece of music. We are listening to a symphony, a song, or even some techno, yet are we listening to all of it, right now? Well, no, we are hearing some notes now. Presumably we must also be remembering or holding in our mind other notes, in order to identify the melody, the rhythm, the movement. Or must we?

St Augustine, he of the 'Lord, make me chaste – but not yet' request, said, 'What then is time? If no one asks me, I know what it is. If I wish to explain it to him who asks, I do not know.'

Well, even when no one asks me, I fear I do not know what time is. What is it, though, that we are seeking to know? Presumably, we seek more explanation, yet in order to explain quite what? After all, just because in the abstract we can talk of dividing any duration again and again – infinitely so – must it therefore be possible to impose such divisions on time and our experience of time, and then also be possible to undo the resultant tangles in our thinking? A comment from Wittgenstein in a different context is, 'The difficulty here is: to stop.'

I stop – just in time.

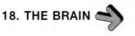

18. THE BRAIN

31. DO WE MAKE THE STARS?

26. BEAUTY AWAKE

5

MAN WITH PULLEY: WAVING
OR DROWNING?

We may wonder whether the girl at sea is waving or drowning, though even if drowning, she may be waving for help; and when you look up at the scaffolding, a man about to land on your head, you may reasonably wonder whether he was pushed, blown by the wind – or jumped, having taken a dislike to your panama hat, shortly to be flattened by the fall.

The puzzle is: what do we do when we do something? What is going on when we jump rather than fall, when we deliberately wave at friends rather than have arms automatically flapping when drowning? The puzzle is important for when we do things, we are usually held responsible – in contrast to when things just happen to us, when, for example, we sneeze, blush, or are pushed.

To attain more focus, there is the tale of the irritated soldier who, when asked by the doctor to clench his teeth,

could not resist the retort, 'No, you clench them,' at which he removed his false teeth and popped them onto the desk.

There are different ways whereby bodily parts get moved. Even when the teeth are original and true, a clenching may occur because you do it directly, or because you yank your jaws together with your hands, or because it is an involuntary twitch. Let us zoom in closer to the puzzle.

A man is in bed. When asked to lift his leg, he pulls at a string with his hands, a string which runs through a system of pulleys and is tied to his leg. Hence, he lifts his leg – and no one else is involved. That is one way of his lifting his leg, but he is not lifting it directly. When he raises his leg directly – with no strings attached, no people pulling it, no gale blowing it – what does he do? The leg goes up, but that movement alone does not amount to his directly lifting his leg. If we, so to speak, subtract the fact that his leg goes up, what remains? What makes it his direct lifting?

What do you do when you raise your leg?

There is a tendency, because of the specific example, to compare the successful case of someone who directly raises his leg with the unsuccessful case of someone who cannot, because of injury or being tied down. In unsuccessful cases we may picture the man trying to raise the leg, some effort involved. If we see the effort as muscles tensing, then we may next imagine a man paralysed, so that not even the muscles tense; yet still he tries to move his leg. Trying becomes viewed as a conscious willing, a mental happening. If such mental activity occurs in the odd and unsuccessful cases, when the leg fails to move, we may answer our puzzle, regarding successful cases, by saying: when someone directly raises his leg, a mental activity – a *willing* occurs – which causes the leg's upward movement.

The term 'action' is often used for what we do, 'movement' for the physical change that occurs. The leg moving up, on its own, is a movement; it is an action if brought about not via strings, but directly by the person concerned. Human actions, then, have often been seen as consisting of a mental component – a willing – and the resultant physical movement. This picture, highly influential, is found in the works of Monsieur Descartes, the seventeenth-century 'father' of modern philosophy.

What puzzles me about the 'willing' approach is why so many people readily accept it. Think of the thousands of things you do every day. Have they all involved mental events – little willings? You shouted at your partner, kissed the cat – not a good start to the day – went to work, to college, to a film. You curled your hair round your fingers. You walked across the room, opened this book, sliced the bread, poured the coffee. True, you sometimes wonder about what to do and how to do it; but is it true that, in all your actions, willings must have been involved that caused the movements? That certainly is not obviously true to your experience.

'Ah, there must have been unconscious willings.' But why be so convinced? Further, if willings must occur for bodily movements to be actions, what are we to say about those willings? They are usually thought of as being actions themselves; but if that is so, then it looks as if those willings must be preceded by earlier willings – but then those earlier willings would need to be preceded by earlier ones still. For example, it looks as if your lifting your leg requires you not only to will your leg to move, but also that you will that you will your leg to move – and will that you will that you will … and so on. Something has surely gone wrong.

Suppose the 'willing', as a mental happening, is part of what an action is. What is the content of the willing? What do you will? Do you will that your leg moves? Well, how do you do that? I bet you have no idea how to will a movement of an object – we draw a veil over Uri Geller.

Try this. Stare at an item nearby – a cup, a glass, a pen – however light you want. Concentrate on it. With all your will, try to make it rise, without touching it. I suspect it has not moved. Now, with whatever form of willing you engaged just then, focus it on your leg – concentrate hard – and see if you can will your leg to move. I am confident that such concentration will fail. If a willing occurs when you move your leg, it is not that you will that your leg moves – for that would be ineffectual, as just seen. Also, you do not will that certain neurological changes occur; you do not know how to do that directly. We know how to cause neurological changes indirectly: we move a leg, sure that some neurological changes must have happened – but we did not will them directly to happen. We do not 'do' the neurological changes.

*   *   *

Although we often think and plan what to do, although we often want to do things, although sometimes we try hard to do things, there seems no good reason to believe that typically our actions consist of mental events, of willings, that cause the physical movements. We have been working with a distorting picture, in thinking that we must find some added mental events to the leg's movement. Perhaps an action usually does not require a psychological element that precedes and causes the movement, even though when we fail to do something, some mental trying or willing may have occurred.

What do you do when you raise your leg? Answer: you do nothing except raise your leg. What is involved in that? Answer: your leg goes up. How does that differ from the case with the string and pulleys? Answer: the string and the pulleys – and maybe the pressure of string on the flesh. How does your raising your leg differ from when it goes up in spasm? Answer: in various ways, depending on circumstances; you may be surprised and embarrassed at what has happened. You may apologize to the nurse who was struck by the misbehaving leg, saying, 'Sorry, I don't know why that happened.'

If someone asks you why you raised your leg, you rightly say, in a spasm case, that you did not raise it; it moved of its own accord. When you have directly raised your leg, then you take direct responsibility – and may give reasons for why you did it. 'I was seeing how far I could stretch. I was trying to touch the ceiling.'

Now, as you read these words, raise a leg, wave a hand, or wiggle your ears. If you're in public, people, of course, may stare, wondering if you need help. Simply say, 'Don't mind me, I'm just seeing what I do, when I do what I do – I am, after all, a philosopher philosophizing.'

They may smile kindly – and move away.

⬅ 1. ON THINKING TOO MUCH: HOW NOT TO WIN A PRINCESS'S HAND

9. THE LIFE MODEL: BEAUTY, BURGLARS, ➡ AND BEHOLDERS

23. PAINTINGS, WITHIN AND WITHOUT ➡

11. SLOTHFUL SLOTH SPEAKS: 'WHAT ➡ WILL BE, WILL BE'

6

'HI, I'M SIR ISAAC NEWTON – DON'T MENTION THE APPLES'

'Hi, I'm Sir Isaac Newton – don't mention the apples,' says the man in the bed, waking up, rubbing his eyes with seeming disbelief.

We must suppose this happens quite recently, certainly in no seventeenth century. The words astonish those who hear them – for the man in the bed is just a regular guy, with the slightly irregular name of 'Ossie'. His wife and children are amazed, and then irritated, as they, understandably so, think their Ossie is having them on, pretending to be Newton. Ossie is speaking in flowery old – ye olde – English. He looks around, amazed. 'Where am I? Where are my servants, my books, and alchemy records? What's this strange lantern glowing in the ceiling? How are words being spoken out of this magical box?'

We could go on in this vein, but happily shall not. Suffice it to say that the individual – Ossie – continues, seemingly in all sincerity, to know nothing of his life as Ossie, but manages to say lots about Isaac Newton as if, indeed, he is Isaac Newton, somehow inhabiting poor Ossie's body – as if, indeed, Isaac Newton is living here in Soho, London, and not dead and buried in Westminster Abbey.

At first we assume Ossie is playing a big game. Yes, we all know the story of Newton, who, it was mistakenly claimed, hit on gravity when apples hit upon him. Ossie could have secretly studied Newton's life, practised the sounds of old English, reflected that Newton would be tired of apple jokes, and so on; but could a time come when it is rational to accept that, hey, maybe after all, somehow or other, Newton has been reincarnated? We should then have lost Ossie. Where indeed is Ossie? But that is a different puzzle. Let us focus on the individual here, this Ossie or Newton, the general question, a question of some gravity, being,

Could it be rational to believe that a deceased historical figure is living again?

We speak of 'could', of what is possible. This does not commit us to saying that it will happen or even is likely to happen. We simply wonder about the sheer possibility, whether there is anything contradictory in the idea.

Who is this man who looks like Ossie, yet speaks like Newton and claims to be Newton? Let us call him 'Issie' – just so that we are leaving things open at this stage, concerning who he really is. If Issie really is the reincarnated Isaac Newton, he must at least describe many events of his past as '*I* experimented with this, wrote that' – and so on. He must speak of Newton, himself, in the first person – and let us suppose that Issie does. We may still doubt whether Issie is Isaac Newton; Ossie could have learnt the historical facts, transposing them into the first person.

Suppose Issie speaks of events unknown to anyone living, yet which can be checked. Maybe he speaks of burying some papers and biblical items in a secret vault under King's College Chapel and in a chest buried under an ancient beech tree at the Gog Magog Hills outside Cambridge. Experts examine the sites, find that they have not been disturbed for centuries, dig away, and discover the items. With such evidence – good evidence, surely – maybe we should think, 'Yes, somehow Newton has been reincarnated in Ossie's body. Issie is Isaac Newton.'

Bodily continuity – having the same body over time – is not essential, it seems, for Newton, or for anyone else, to survive. Issie – I mean, Newton – agrees. 'I keep telling you that I am Isaac Newton, though I can't get used to this body which I now find myself with. Ossie didn't keep himself in trim, I can tell only too well.'

But … Consider a further possibility. Unbeknownst to us, Bruce, sleeping on Australia's Bondi Beach, also woke up one afternoon, saying, 'Hi, I'm Sir Isaac Newton – don't mention the apples.' This individual knows nothing about what has been happening regarding Ossie. Bruce goes through similar astonished declarations to those of Issie – maybe greater astonishment in light of the bikini-clad Bondi Beach. To register our uncertainty about the identity of this man whom we thought of as Bruce, but who is now claiming to be Newton, let us call him 'Aussie'. The evidence for Aussie being Newton ends up being just as strong as the evidence for Issie being Newton. So, if we are right in thinking that the evidence showed that Issie was Newton, then we should also believe that Aussie is Newton. If so, we seem committed to the belief that Aussie, the individual in Australia, is identical with Issie, the individual in London. Yet that is surely impossible. How can one and the same person be both in Australia and Britain at the same time, knowing nothing of what each other is doing? Has Newton been reincarnated as a split personality inhabiting two different bodies?

*   *   *

We could, without logical contradiction, have twenty-seven, or twenty-seven thousand, such individuals all waking up, announcing sincerely that they are Newton, all with equally strong credentials. With the single awakening, the Issie case alone, it seems reasonable to believe that Newton is alive and well. With the multiple cases, we should be baffled. The mere possibility of the multiple cases does not count against Newton being reincarnated in the single case. But although that is true, the possibility of multiple cases does appear to count against psychological conditions alone being sufficient for what it is for one and the same person to be reincarnated.

Let us return to the single case of Issie. Let us assume that Issie is indeed Isaac Newton. If so, then Issie might have been Newton even though he was unable to give any impressive evidence about buried papers to establish the fact, not least because he, Newton, performed no such burials. We – and Newton – hit lucky with our reincarnated Newton; he possessed distinctive knowledge to pass on. We also hit lucky because he was not confused; he knew who he was – but it is possible for a person still to be the same person yet to have forgotten a huge amount about his identity. Suppose Newton, when he awoke in Ossie's body, was having his own psychological problems. Just as he, so to speak, invaded Ossie's body, so he, Newton, felt that his mind was being invaded, an odd collection of mistaken memories, thoughts, and attitudes, squeezing out his own ...

And so it is possible – or is it? – that our tale could have coherently been of Newton waking up in Ossie's body, utterly confused who he was. Indeed, if we dare press logical conceivability even further, may not poor Newton have woken up in Ossie's body, even more confused, thinking himself to be a man called 'Ossie', waking up in the twenty-first century. If so, then, as we nod to a man in a bed, humouring a poor and possibly confused Ossie – as we see him – in fact the man in the bed is Sir Isaac, unaware of who he really is.

And so it is that we learn that we should not push possibilities too far, yet the puzzle then is: how far is too far?

18. THE BRAIN

26. BEAUTY AWAKE

**28. COCKTAILS, RIVERS, AND
SIR JOHN CUTLER'S STOCKINGS**

7

SHOULD WE SAVE THE JERBOA?

The long-eared jerboa has – er – long ears. It lives in the deserts of Mongolia and China – with its ears. A tiny nocturnal mammal, it is dwarfed by enormous ears. It hops like a kangaroo; and, for mammals, it possesses one of the biggest ear-to-body ratios. That is, it has very big ears for its size. There are little hairs on its feet, almost like snow shoes, which allow the jerboa to jump along the sand. It is said to be cute and comic. It is classified as endangered. Oh, and did I mention the ears?

Why should we care about the jerboa? Our question is about the species, as a kind, or a class of creatures. A species is easily confused in speech with the individual members of the species, not least because our language so easily flips around: 'the jerboa' could designate a particular jerboa, or the species taken to be a group of jerboas, or the species taken to be the type of creature it is. Individual jerboas have

two long ears each, but the species, as a collection, does not really have long ears and certainly not merely two, though the species as a type of creature is that type that normally has two long ears. When people are concerned about a species' survival, they usually want to promote the existence of a collection of creatures of a certain type, but not any individuals in particular. Particular individuals die, but the species, the collection with members of a certain type, may persist.

Naturally, we may also care about individual jerboas: probably we do not want any individual jerboa to suffer. We recognize that there is something that counts as going well for an individual jerboa. But the species, as a species, is not the sort of thing that suffers pain. Preserving a species may, in fact, involve culling, killing some members. So our general question is – and a couple of examples are –

Why save a species from extinction?

Why save the jerboa?

Why regret the loss of the dodo?

Some simple quick answers in favour of preservation concern the benefits or possible benefits to humans. Preservation is justified on the grounds of the species' value as an instrument to aid us. Perhaps the different species help maintain Earth's ecological balance. Maybe their genetic information, one day, could aid development of pharmaceuticals. In addition, people gain pleasure from seeing members of different species. For similar reasons, we may regret the loss of the dodo.

Suppose the jerboa lacks such instrumental value with regard to ecology and future genetic researches. Suppose too that the jerboa is so furtive, living in such inhospitable conditions, that people typically will not see a jerboa and so will not gain pleasure from sighting experiences. May the species yet possess value?

Yes. People may value simply knowing that the jerboa exists, knowing that there is such a species and such variety around them. We are identifying a curious instrumental value, curious in that it fails to involve our direct experiences of the jerboa. Once again, though, we are finding value in the jerboa's existence because of its effects on humans, albeit not directly experienced effects. However, may the jerboa, or any species, have an intrinsic value, a value that does not depend for its being a value on something else – that does not depend, for example, on what humans want?

The question does not presuppose that a species cannot have both instrumental value and intrinsic value. This is not an either–or matter. Some items have both. Philosophizing, arguably, is intrinsically valuable, yet may also possess instrumental value in bringing peace and harmony to the universe. Well, okay – maybe that last point is a little fanciful. What is not fanciful is the thought that some things have intrinsic value. Somewhere along the line we stop ourselves from saying 'this is only valuable because it is a means to that ...' For example, the stopping point is often happiness, usually human happiness: happiness has intrinsic value.

Returning to the jerboa, by pretending that it lacks all instrumental value, we focus on whether there is any other value, an intrinsic value, that applies to the species. Perhaps there is value in the jerboa's existence simply because it is a species of living individuals. Well, it is not obviously the case that 'living' thereby makes something valuable. The smallpox virus, HIV, and malarial mosquitoes are living, yet we question whether they are thereby intrinsically valuable. Our negative attitude, though, may result from their harming us: they could still be intrinsically valuable.

Possibly there is something valuable about nature being left, undisturbed by human beings; however, that certainly does not point to species' conservation. Nature ensures the extinction of vast numbers of species – and it may be in our human nature, quite whatever that means, to destroy species, just as it is to tame parts of nature. The rural landscapes of fields, crops, and national parks would be non-existent, but for human interferences – as would be spectacular bridges, sculptures, and architecturally stunning galleries.

*   *   *

Perhaps we should simply recognize that we value the presence of a variety of species. We value that presence independently of our purposes and independently of any value for us. We value the jerboa for its own sake. Note, though, that even here its value may be resting solely on the fact that we humans value it 'for its own sake'. There is, though, a stronger suggestion: that the jerboa – or any species – possesses value independently even of our valuing it. After all, if the species in question did not possess such value, why should we value it for its own sake? Why value something unless it is worthy of being valued?

It is difficult, though, to get a grip on 'for its own sake' when applied to a species. If we do something for an individual jerboa's sake, we have some idea of how we are acting in its best interests, how its life may go well. We know that it needs food and shelter. But it is far from clear that a species, as opposed to particular individuals, has an interest. It is far from clear how things go well for the species, from the species' viewpoint. After all, a species lacks a viewpoint.

Human beings promote the existence of some things and not of others. We value. We are *valuers*. Perhaps – and perhaps conveniently for human beings – possessors of intrinsic value include at least those individuals that are themselves valuers, such as we are. We may, though, wonder why that should be believed. Without valuers, nothing would be valued; but it neither follows that valuers are valuable nor that items are only valuable if they happen to be valued.

In our valuing, having preferences, recognizing things as worthy of desire, perhaps we become aware that there are items that are intrinsically valuable, whose value is other than being experienced by us or even being experiences. Maybe that is why so many of us, even when godless, stand in wonder at the different species, seeking to preserve them against the ravages of both man and impersonal nature. Maybe that is why some of us see beauty in sunsets, in landscapes, and seascapes, a beauty that is valuable and would still exist even without humans around to appreciate that beauty.

In some cases, it may be better not to have human beings around at all. Just think of those seashores splattered with empty beer cans, cigarette ends, and worse. They offend the eye and detract from beauty; yet, without the humans around, could there be any offence, any loss or gain in beauty at all?

Or would the eye of the universe still shed a tear?

9. THE LIFE MODEL: BEAUTY, BURGLARS, AND BEHOLDERS

22. VEILS OF WOE: BEATS AND PEEPING TOMS TOO

33. FRAGILE CREATURES THAT WE ARE ...

8

WHEN ONE MAKES TWO: DRESSING UP

Variety is the spice of life – or so it is said. Maybe that saying leads a few to change their identities. More often the change has evasion in mind, perhaps because of bigamy charges, evasion of tax, or police in pursuit. Avoiding embarrassment can motivate changes in names – parents, take care when naming your young. Some changes are turnings on pathways to fame: Norma Jean became Marilyn Monroe. Or, for that matter, they occur after seeing the light: bound to Damascus, Saul became Paul. Yet double lives become the outcome for some – and such lives may spell some logical trouble.

David delights in variety; he delights so much that he often dresses in a womanly fashion – as Lady Davinia – playing the lady role exceptionally well. When out in public, and not dressed as Davinia, he is masculine and mean – 'Dave', so rough and so tough. The girls swoon at Dave the tough, yet are unmoved by Davinia the cool. Men dismiss Dave as 'Jack the Lad', but yearn for kisses from Davinia so cool, so elegant. David's changes in persona always take place in private. People, if observing his apartment, often see Dave, dressed in the usual leathers, disappearing indoors; sometime later, Lady Davinia appears, her long blonde hair shimmering, dress sparkling and stilettos so sharp.

Many things, it seems, are true of Davinia, yet not of Dave. Men open car doors for Davinia, but never for Dave. On particular occasions, Dave, not Davinia, enters the home; later Davinia, not Dave, exits. We may add complexity by commenting about David, but allow him to drop out of the picture, until required again. Consider how we may reason:

1. Girls make dates with Dave.
2. Dave is Davinia.
3. So, girls make dates with Davinia.

Claims (1) and (2) are readily accepted as true, yet we – even we in the know – may well resist agreeing that claim (3) is true too. After all, girls do not really date Davinia. Yet if they do not, we hit the puzzle that follows:

As Dave and Davinia are one individual, how can some things true of Dave not be true of Davinia?

We may have wanted to ask, 'How can some things be true of one, yet not of the other?' – but, while we have the 'one', we lack the 'another'. 'They' are one and the same person, identified by two names. If we have two names for the same item and know which item that is, we can surely substitute one name for the other, without altering the truth of what we say. Lewis Carroll was Charles Dodgson. It is a truth that Dodgson died in 1898; so it must surely also be true that Carroll died in the same year.

One line of thought, the Identity Line, stresses that the same things really are true of Dave and Davinia. The line needs, then, to explain why we tend mistakenly to think otherwise. Another line, the Difference Line, accepts that there really are some differences between what is true of Dave and of Davinia – and that is because we misunderstand use of the names.

According to one Difference Line, everything that persists is really a sequence of temporal stages. Why it is true that girls swoon at Dave and not at Davinia is because the temporal stages differ: the Dave stages differ from the Davinia stages. In claims (1) and (3), we are not directly referring to the same individual, but to a person's different stages in time: a 'Dave' stage in (1); a 'Davinia' stage in (3).

In criticism of this Difference Line, is a continuing life really just a sequence of temporal stages? Maybe it is, when natural and significant developments occur. Yes, the tadpole is a temporal stage of a creature that has the later stage of frog. David, though, keeps switching between Dave and Davinia: the temporal stages of Dave lack continuity. For that matter,

David, the generator of the persona changes, would also need to be fitted into the temporal tale.

The Difference Line demands linguistic juggling. It is not obviously true that girls swoon at temporal stages of a man. More accurately, it is not obviously true that female stages swoon at male stages. Maybe 'swooning' needs understanding afresh. Further, perhaps girls speak to rough-voiced Dave on a mobile, while peering through the apartment's curtains, seeing Davinia on the phone. That is, David is dressed as Davinia, yet speaking as Dave: the temporal stage is the same, yet both Dave and Davinia are present. The Difference Line also needs to explain why claim (2), Dave is Davinia, seems true. Perhaps 'is' sometimes needs special rendering as 'is a temporal stage of the same person as'. Yes, much juggling is required.

The Difference Line is problematic. How fares the Identity Line? This line keeps faith with the thought that Dave and Davinia really are the same individual. So why do we make different assessments about what is true of them? Maybe claim (3), 'Girls make dates with Davinia', is true; but we resist assent because assent would mislead people unaware that Davinia is David, and that David is appearing as Dave, whenever girls date him.

Here is an analogy. I speak the truth in saying that the Queen appeared on television and was sober. If however I make that comment, you may wrongly conclude that she is not usually sober. Why would anyone mention her sobriety,

unless it was unusual? Even though what I say does not logically imply that the Queen is usually drunk, my comment may
convey an alcoholic royalty. A little similarly, we hesitate in
announcing that claim (3) is true because we realize how, in
many contexts, to assert it would mislead. Here, of course,
we have already exposed David's lifestyle; so, here, asserting
claim (3) as true should not mislead. More explanations are
therefore needed; and more problems duly arise.

*   *   *

We want to say that girls do not date Dave *as Davinia*. Girls
make dates with Davinia, not as Davinia, but *as Dave*. Maybe
claim (1) is truthfully saying, or implying, that girls make
dates with someone personified as Dave – with claim (3)
falsely saying that they make dates with someone personified
as Davinia. This line seems to make the strange commitment
that girls make dates with personifications or aspects. Can
you date a persona or aspect? If David's cross-dressing ways
are revealed, girls may truthfully say, 'Wow, so sometimes
Dave is dressed as Davinia, a woman.' But that does not
amount to saying that David personified as Dave is sometimes
dressed as David personified as Davinia. David, when personified as Dave, certainly is not dressed as Davinia.

The above approaches to the cross-dressing puzzle generate more and more difficulties. Perhaps we fail to see the
wood for the trees, even though – dare I say? – the wood is
identical with a collection of trees. The puzzle has arisen

because we have two different names and a story – a story that provides two different sets of thoughts and pictures, one set associated with one name, the other set with the other name. We hold two separate files on David, for we know about the double life. Which file we handle depends upon which name is being used.

'Do girls make dates with Davinia? – yes or no.' Resist being bullied into giving a 'yes' or a 'no'. Let our answer be, 'In a way, yes; and, in a way, no.'

'Did you meet your husband before you married him?'

'Yes.'

'So, he was your husband when you met him?'

'No.'

Let us try the question again. 'Did you meet your husband before you married him?'

'Well, no.'

'So, you just went and married a perfect stranger, you poor thing. I'm so sorry.'

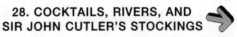

28. COCKTAILS, RIVERS, AND SIR JOHN CUTLER'S STOCKINGS

20. HOW TO GAIN WHATEVER YOU WANT

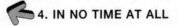

4. IN NO TIME AT ALL

31. DO WE MAKE THE STARS?

9

THE LIFE MODEL: BEAUTY, BURGLARS, AND BEHOLDERS

A burglar is set on robbing an apartment. He could knock at the door and announce his intentions, but that makes the burglary unlikely to succeed. He needs first to case the joint; so he pretends to be a window cleaner. Of course, just turning up, saying he is a window cleaner, would be suspicious. He needs a story – at least, a bucket, ladder, and some more. With the required equipment in place, he climbs the ladder and peers through the windows, to establish the jewellery's location. People are wandering in and out of the rooms; so, again to avoid suspicion, he makes as if he is washing the windows, yet he senses the occupants may be un-fooled. Playing safe, he starts washing the windows properly, and then proceeds to give them a fine shine. Of course, he is only pretending to clean the windows – and yet he is cleaning the windows.

This little puzzle is readily solved: he is pretending to be a window cleaner while really cleaning the windows. Complexities arise if he really is a window cleaner as well as burglar. The tale reminds us that what happens, where people are involved, depends not solely on physical movements, but also on intentions and context. Let us keep that reminder in mind, as we move to a puzzle.

'A group of clothed men are staring intensely at an attractive naked young woman, stretched out before them.' Someone, not in the know, describes the scene thus. Yet the men and woman would reject that description. We are at a life class; painting is about to take place.

Of course, models are sometimes men and artists women; but, to avoid repeated caveats, here we have a female model and heterosexual male artists. The woman may, indeed, be modest, someone who normally dresses very conservatively, who would not dream of flaunting herself. She may, indeed, be suspicious of window cleaners. In a painter's studio, though, things are different: the artists seek the aesthetic. The artists would probably be indignant, were they perceived as delighting in her nakedness, as if in a strip club. To suggest a sexual element displays an uncouth character, a failure to grasp the difference between the nude as ideal and the naked or bare. After all, naked truth and bare-faced lies are neither nude truth nor nude-faced lies. The nude is distinctive, a beautiful art form; the gaze an aesthetic gaze. Yet:

How divorced is the artistic gaze from the real world of desire?

Sometimes the aesthetic realm is seen as ethereal, separate from desire, at least of an earthly ilk. Of course, nudes were sometimes painted expressly for bedchambers, calculated to excite lustful feelings; but, focusing on the aesthetics of the nude, a detached attitude, it is said, is required by viewers, as by artists when creating the paintings. The model and the nude in the painting are to be viewed for their form. Then, there is no shame of our prying, no lascivious thoughts. The aesthetic experience may even ennoble.

Ignoring whether art needs to be of the beautiful, let us focus on those many cases where 'beautiful' would be a natural expression for what is seen, where there is talk of curves and contours, balance and harmony, shadings and textures. The beautiful here need not amount to the good-looking. Rembrandt's paintings are often beautiful, even if the subjects are some distance from good looking.

One traditional approach is that beauty is indeed not in beholders' eyes, but resides in certain mathematical proportions, objectively present. Musical harmonies are simple arithmetical ratios between lengths of vibrating strings. Analogously, there are, it has been said, underlying harmonies in beautiful paintings – and this applies to the nudes. Even recently it has been suggested that such beauty, with its harmony, promotes a sense of justice. Of course, it cannot simply be a matter of harmony; harmony is sometimes merely boring. Also, the simple may be beautiful, yet be so simple that it lacks parts to be in harmony.

Whatever the details, there results, it is claimed, a distinctive aesthetic appreciation of the nude, far removed from sexual desire. And so, both sexes can appreciate the beauty of proportion in human bodies and their representation. The desire to experience the beauty of the nude is a disinterested desire. A clear difference exists between, for example, the enjoyment aroused by pornography or photographs of glamour models and those by paintings of nudes, even though the scenes portrayed may be similar. A clear difference exists between a burglar pretending to be a window cleaner and a real window cleaner, even when in both cases the windows get cleaned.

Aesthetic appreciation involves pleasure. When we find nudes beautiful, we experience certain pleasurable sensations, even sensual; and presumably those sensations depend on our biology. Were we disembodied, spiritual, in some non-earthly realm, yet viewing the paintings, could we experience the beauty? Perhaps we could be intellectually aware of the harmonies – but would not appreciation require bodily sensations? Could we sense a sunset's beauty, yet without pleasurable feelings? Simply measuring lines and recognizing proportions do not thereby generate aesthetic appreciation. The body, the feelings, the emotions, are essential to our awareness of the beautiful – bringing us back down to earth. In particular, our sexual constitution would seem to have something to do with which curves and flesh tones are thought beautiful – be it because we identify with them or seek them. If so, the aesthetic delights that men take in female nudes may not be so utterly divorced from other feelings, feelings not directly associated with the eye. However, this fact – if it is a fact – can lead people to draw mistaken conclusions.

One mistaken conclusion concerns beauty. People often conclude that the beautiful is relative to our biological make-up. Whether gin is nice depends on 'nice *for whom*'; whether something is beautiful – well, that depends on 'beautiful *for whom*'. Indeed, evolutionary psychologists, ever fond of the 'just', sometimes say that beautiful features are *just* those indicative of health; being drawn to the beautiful is *nothing but* being drawn to the healthy, to hand down our genes. I urge resistance to the relativity claim, to the 'just' and 'nothing but'. Compare with the following.

Probably there is a good evolutionary explanation of why we, evolutionary survivors, can distinguish shapes from colours, land from sea – yet the differences between shapes and colours, land and sea, are not *just* their evolutionary utility. Our biology is required for our awareness of the world and its features; it does not follow that the world and its features depend on our biology. So, too, with beauty: just because we need a certain biology to recognize beauty it does not follow that beauty depends on that biology.

* * *

As biology has some role in aesthetic appreciation, people sometimes also mistakenly conclude, not just that beauty is relative, but that the aesthetic gaze by males is *really* or *nothing but* a sexual yearning. It is as if there is no real difference between lusting after someone and appreciating the beauty. The analogous mistake would be to think that there is no real difference between a burglar and window cleaner, when both are cleaning the windows.

Differences exist between lusting and appreciating, though differences are sometimes a matter of degree and sometimes intermingled. Artists, for example, have often seduced their models, even claiming aesthetic impulse. Yet models who sit for genuine life classes should not be sitting as objects of lust. If an artist's primary concern is lust – he pretends to draw, or even draws, as a burglar pretends to clean windows and cleans windows – then he is engaged in deception as is the burglar. He is mistreating the model, even if she reclines, unaware of his intentions and desires.

None of this is to deny that muddles occur over what is really happening and what matters, when perceptions enter the fray. 'What is that man at the window, or in the artist's studio, really doing?' Think of actors: when acting their parts, they rarely pretend to walk; they walk. They are pretending, say, to cross hills, when really they cross the stage. They do not pretend to kiss and caress, for they do kiss and caress; and yet, because of the context, the kiss and caress lack the significance of kisses and caresses in reality – or often do.

Suppose an actor plays against an actress who happens to be his real-life wife with whom he is angry in real life. And, in the play, the actress plays the part of a wife and he plays that of the angry husband – then where do acting and reality separate? What is really going on depends on intentions, on context, on the bigger picture – and yet are we not also pulled towards thinking that we can tell part of what is really going on without the bigger picture?

After all, the windows do get cleaned.

23. PAINTINGS, WITHIN AND WITHOUT ➥

16. 'MY BELOVED IS MINE' *or* **'THE TROUBLE WITH FOOTBALL IS THE OTHER TEAM'** ➥

19. WHAT'S WRONG WITH EATING PEOPLE? *or even* **WHO'S FOR DINNER?** ➥

⬅ **5. MAN WITH PULLEY: WAVING OR DROWNING?**

10

AN OFFER YOU CAN ONLY REFUSE

Some offers, it is quipped, *The Godfather* in mind, are offers you cannot refuse. What may be seen as kindly offers, by those in the know, are nothing but mean and nasty threats or tricks – but no treats at all. When the gunman asks you to unlock the safe, well, were you to play for time, pondering the invitation, you know without doubt that your health is at risk. When cops solicit your company down at the station – 'A few questions, sir' – it would be foolish and pointless to decline their kindly request.

There are, though, offers that you can only refuse – or, more accurately, they cannot logically be accepted. I apologize for introducing illness again, but suppose you feel unwell, rotten, and feeble; so, off to the doctor's you go. To your surprise, she gives you a choice of cure.

There's no problem in making you better. There are two ways to health. You could either take this medicine four times a day for a week. True, it tastes nasty and may well give you headaches; but you'll definitely get better. Here's an alternative. Simply believe that you'll get better. What's wrong with you merely requires your belief that you will be well; the belief is as effective as the medicine. No need, then, for the nasty medicine. And this is not mumbo-jumbo. There's vast evidence that beliefs often aid recovery; after all, beliefs have some basis in states of the brain and brain states affect the rest of the body.

The doctor smiles; she adds that the 'belief' option is surely the rational one to choose. You agree: obviously you would rather follow the recommended belief route, thereby avoiding the medicinal. Yet can you simply choose to believe something? Is not that an impossible offer to take up? Beliefs cannot just be turned on at will.

Let us, then, revise our medicinal tale a little. You accept the medicine, believing it will make you better. In fact, unbeknownst to you, it lacks all curative properties in itself – and the doctor knows this. Perhaps it is just water – with an additive that provides the nasty taste and colour. It is a placebo. Its sole role in the explanation of how patients become better is that they falsely believe its chemical composition possesses curative powers; and so they believe they will get better. It is this latter belief that then causes the recovery. Now, the doctor may truthfully murmur what she knows to be true:

> The medicine will make my patient better only in so far as he believes it will make him better.

If you overhear the comment, believing the doctor to be truthful, then you are now about to believe:

The medicine will make me better only in so far as I believe it will make me better.

Yet, in the circumstances given, you cannot believe that – well, not rationally so. Paradoxically, the doctor can, but you cannot, believe the truth about the matter – a paradox of self-believing.

Why should learning the truth about your belief undermine that truth?

You believed that the medicine would make you better because of its pharmaceutical powers. Learning that it lacks such powers, you lack the belief that it will make you better; hence, you lack the resultant belief that you will get better. Lacking the belief, you obviously cannot get better because of the belief.

The Placebo Paradox, here on display, arises because what is true cannot survive, cannot remain true, upon your discovery. So long as you do not discover that the medicine is a placebo, your belief that you will get better is true. Upon discovery, if only you could hang onto your belief that you will get better, all would be well in your getting well; and hence your belief would be true. The discovery, though, pulls the rug from under your belief. Your belief that you would get better was grounded solely by belief in the medicine; with that grounding, that reason, now gone, your belief has gone too.

In contrast, the doctor's belief that you would get better was grounded on the efficacy of patients' believing they get better through, for example, taking placebos not believed to be placebos. Now, an optimistic patient, without placebos, may believe in any case that he will recover; but his belief that he will recover, while the reason why he does recover, cannot logically be the reason for his *belief* that he will recover. Your believing that so and so cannot be the reason for your believing that so and so. A reason needs to be different from what it is a reason for.

In fact, placebo prescriptions can work even when patients learn placebos are prescribed and know what 'placebo' means. Our paradox, though, set off with you, the patient, believing that you will recover because of the efficacy of the medicine – for that reason alone.

* * *

The Placebo Paradox has something of a self-defeating air. If you learn why you will get better, then you will not get better, given the circumstances set out. The learning defeats, so to speak, what is learnt. The paradox does not involve some simple self-defeating in the way that shouting out 'No one is shouting' is self-defeating. It may be more akin to that of a schoolgirl being told that she is very bright and will pass the examination; this leads to her over-confidence, or indeed nerves, such that she subsequently fails the examination.

A reason for a belief, to be a reason, needs in some way to be independent of that belief. Religious believers sometimes justify belief on the basis of scripture. 'But why believe the scriptures?' 'Because they are God's word.' 'Why believe that?' 'Because it says so in the scriptures.'

Reasons offered in support of beliefs need to stand independently of the beliefs and not themselves be supported by those beliefs. Independence can be important in various ways. In health, for example, if told that your heart is fine, you would reasonably think that your life was not about to be cut short because of your heart – that any early death would at least be initiated by some factors not dependent on a poor heart. With that sensible thought in mind, we may spot the ambiguity and wit in a splendid W. C. Fields' quip. Here it comes.

'Don't worry about your heart; it will last you as long as you live.'

17. GOD, CHOCOLATE, AND NEWCOMB: TAKE THE BOX?

27. THE GREATEST MIRACLE?

32. WITHOUT END?

11

SLOTHFUL SLOTH SPEAKS: 'WHAT WILL BE, WILL BE'

Meeting a sloth, deep in sloth, and a butterfly, fluttering by in a South American jungle, is no surprise, but hearing the name of a Roman orator, Cicero, dropped into the conversation – well, how could I resist listening? I had been hacking through creepers, heat, and undergrowth, perspiration pouring, so, in any case, I needed a rest.

'But, but, but,' said Flutterby, settling on Sloth's snout, 'being so slothful and lazy, why, you may starve to death, whatever you've been reading in Cicero.'

'What will be, will be,' sighed Sloth, hanging upside down from a branch.

'That may well be so,' buttered Flutterby, 'But what will be, does not *have* to be.'

Sloth sighed, slothfully of course, but the butterfly tickled him into saying more.

'Look,' said Sloth, 'If it's fated that I shall dine this after-

YOU'RE JUST GOING TO HANG AROUND AND LET FATE DECIDE IF YOU EAT OR NOT?

THE ANSWER IS ON THE TIP OF MY TONGUE...

noon, then I shall dine, whether I go hunting for food or not. If it's fated that I shall starve, then I shall starve, whether or not I go hunting for food.'

'Ah, the Lazy Argument,' interrupted Flutterby. Sloth, though, was in full, albeit slow slothful flow.

'And either it is fated that I shall dine this afternoon or it is fated that I shall not. So, either way, it is a waste of energy to go searching for dinner.'

'You should have read more Cicero,' fluttered the butter-fly, 'for fallacy rests in your reasoning.' And in her excitement, she fluttered around, landing on Sloth's outstretched tongue. As Sloth gulped her down, I heard him murmur with a satisfied yawn, 'So, clearly it was fated I'd have at least a teeny hors-d'oeuvre.'

If it is true that things are going to happen, are we not powerless to prevent them?

When in times of distress, despair or even guilt, we may sigh, 'What will be, will be.' People sing the words, often in Spanish tongues, 'Que sera, sera.' Such sighs, such songs, such tongues, may manifest hopelessness. We cannot affect the future. Or, if we are sighing over the past, there was nothing that we could have done to have made things turn out differently. The events in question are fixed – determined by the stars or hand of fate, or some sort of divine predestination.

'Don't bother to smarten up for the interview. After all, either you'll get the job or you won't.' 'There's no need to revise for the examination. Either I'll pass or I won't. Let's party instead.' Such reasoning has, indeed, been well-named: the Lazy Argument.

Is it true that what will be will be? If it is, does it lead to fatalism, the belief that certain things are going to happen regardless of how much we try to prevent or encourage them? If or when you meet, or fail to meet, the man or woman of your dreams, was it just meant to be?

Showing fatalism to be true cannot be as easy as muttering, singing, or sighing, 'What will be, will be' – and, nodding wisely, grasping how true that is. True, if something will be, then it will be. If something will happen, then it will happen. But the butterfly is right: it is not at all obviously true that we are all fated, that we cannot affect the future. What will be will be – true. What will be, *must* be – well, that is a radically different claim, one that has not yet been justified. Sloth's Lazy Argument, though, seems to have more going for it than the weary sigh of 'what will be, will be'. Here is another example of his lazy reasoning.

> You are ill. Well, either it is fated that you'll recover or it is fated that you'll not recover. If it is fated that you'll recover, then there's no need to bother visiting the doctor. If it is fated that you'll not recover, then it's pointless visiting the doctor. Either it's fated that you'll recover or fated that you will not. Either way, don't waste time visiting the doctor.

As it stands, this can hardly be welcomed as a good argument for fatalism; after all, it assumes straight off that things are fated – either you are fated to recover or fated not to recover. Why believe that?

*   *   *

We are, though, being unfair to Sloth. Here is a modified Lazy Argument.

> Either you are going to recover from the illness or you are not going to recover. If you're going to recover, then there's

no need to see the doctor. If you're not going to recover, then it's pointless seeing the doctor. Either way, therefore, don't waste time seeing the doctor.

Well, what do we make of that? For a start, it does not presuppose fate.

There are many events over which we are powerless. Whatever we do, we shall not affect the orbit of Pluto, the nature of snow, and the colours of rainbows. You and I are unlikely to find a reliable plumber late at night or make the trains run on time. But surely we often do influence our recovery from an illness, getting a job, or passing an examination.

The Lazy Argument's simple mistake is to assume that if something is going to happen, then it is going to happen regardless of what we do. Maybe it is true that we are going to recover from the illness; but this may be because we do see the doctor. Of course, some of us, sceptics that we are, think that recovery is more likely if we avoid doctors. Perhaps you are going to be offered the job after the interview, but only because you do polish your shoes, sound eager, and smile brightly at the boss's jokes. Perhaps you will find the lover of your dreams, but finding her or him is more likely if you keep your eyes open.

'What will be, will be' does not logically lead to 'what will be, will be, whatever you or I do'. Concerning many factors that affect our lives, we cannot pass the responsibility buck to fate. We do have inputs, though it is true that few inputs guarantee desired outcomes.

If we want to avoid responsibility for what happens, we should have more success turning to the unexpected events that hit us in life – the chances, the contingencies, the good or bad luck – rather than to some mysterious notion of fate. Indeed, your chancing upon the Lazy Argument may tempt you to try it out, when looking into his or her eyes, declaring that your getting together was simply fated to be – and so all resistance is futile.

Good luck.

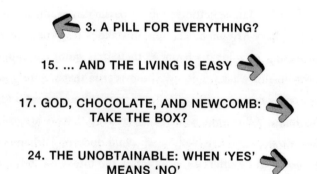

← 3. A PILL FOR EVERYTHING?

15. ... AND THE LIVING IS EASY →

17. GOD, CHOCOLATE, AND NEWCOMB: →
TAKE THE BOX?

24. THE UNOBTAINABLE: WHEN 'YES' →
MEANS 'NO'

12

'WOMEN AND MEN ARE EQUAL' – REALLY?

Where is the equality? The female differs from the male, the average woman differs from the average man – and individual women differ from individual men. They differ biologically, differing in their genes, reproductive features, and likely lifespans. True, individual men and women have features in common simply because they are human. True, although the average woman and man vary in height, weight, and shoe size – in tearful propensities, sexual preferences, and shopping desires – in these respects some individual women and men are equal. In view of the biology, it should be no surprise that the average woman and man differ emotionally, intellectually, and perceptually in many respects. Individual men differ from individual men, women from women, and women from men – in numerous ways.

Talk of sexual equality is typically shorthand, or short-talk, for saying that women and men *should* be treated equally

– that equal treatment is justified. Yet equal treatment should no more be dished out to women and men than to the healthy and unhealthy. Individuals with broken legs rightly need treatment, but those with unbroken legs do not; if they demand it, they may need a different treatment – from psychiatrists. It would be crazy to screen men for cervical cancer or women for prostate cancer. These are but reminders that treating the sexes differently is often the right thing to do.

The puzzle is quite what constitutes sexual equality and what justifies the demand for it? Another way of raising the matter, with both a general and a particular question, is to ask:

Which differences between women and men should be retained?

Should men receive preferential treatment to equalize female/male average lifespans?

The call for sexual equality is probably for an equal concern for both males and females, and their roles in society. That equal concern is often restricted to some sort of equality in opportunities rather than outcome, yet they are sometimes entangled.

Typically, there is no good reason to promote the lives of one sex over the other – though occasionally there is. In a declining population, encouraging women to bear children may be a high priority, suggesting more resources for females than males. If couples are reluctant to have children, then there may be good reason to provide incentives for child-bearing. These are not thereby examples of equal concern for both women and men. They would justify inequalities in treatment on the basis of a value such as society's continuance or requiring sufficient people of working age to support others. Also, they would not necessarily benefit women; they may be pressurizing some women who would prefer childless lives. In some countries, we witness opposite pressures, with childbearing being restricted.

A simple point here is that sexual equality, quite whatever it is, does not always merit highest priority. Further, equal concern for lives faring well does not mean that lives should fare well in the same way. Some men want children; some do not. Some women do; some do not. We still have not, then, discovered the heart of the 'sexual equality' demand, if intended to be more than equal concern for lives, regardless of gender.

Sometimes the equality demand is linked to proportions: things are wrong when the female–male ratio in the same occupation or college course radically differs from fifty-fifty. Many feminist-minded women rail at societies where more women than men typically stay at home, raising children, without paid careers. Yet why ever assume that numerical equality is how things should be? Perhaps there is something in the biology that accounts for such differences; and perhaps there is nothing wrong in that.

Perhaps there is nothing wrong, but there could be something wrong. The numerical differences may result, not from biology, but from unfairness or coercion.

Unfairness first. Whatever the exact biological differences, there is no obvious good reason why, for example, one sex should have the vote but not the other. However, whether there should be numerical equality between the sexes in parliaments, congresses, and senates is a different matter. If representative bodies should reflect citizens represented, should we not ensure the 'right' parliamentary proportions of philosophers, homosexuals, ballet lovers, even criminals – and, indeed, regardless of people's votes? The call for equality between the sexes among representatives suggests that women and men, as groups, possess some significantly different concerns. Paradoxically, this particular call for sexual equality is probably justified by some important sexual inequalities, inequalities not needing eradication.

Returning to employment, if women are rejected for jobs simply 'because they are women', then that is usually unfair. However, it is not unfair if, for example, the drama requires male actors. It is not unfair to men if beauty salons prefer employing women, conscious of clients preferring the female touch. Of course, if women and men do the same work, then they deserve equal pay. If – *if* – society, though, has customs, even legislation, whereby it is far more likely that women, rather than men, will disrupt their employed careers for child-rearing, then it is not obviously unfair for employers to prefer equally good candidates lacking such future disruption dangers. Or is it?

Such discriminatory practices may be unfair if women are forced or customarily expected to have children; coercion is touched on below. The practices may be unfair if it is simply assumed that 'because they are women' the individuals concerned are bound therefore to want children and disrupt careers. They may not; and perhaps this could be established. However – at least on the surface – many women and men, without coercion, simply want to have children. Further, as a matter of biology, women will, therefore, usually have more time away from work than men, which, but for special provision, is likely to affect their careers. So, it would seem, many are arguing that fairness in such cases requires that special allowances be made for women in such circumstances.

Once we enter the arena of justifying allowances – an arena we are bound to enter – it is pretty difficult to find firm groundings. Here is a silly example. Some people may really want to be fire-fighters, yet seriously lack the appropriate stamina. Presumably no one truly believes that such individuals should be specially catered for, perhaps by providing special fitness training, drugs, and reduced duties. However, some people are more prone to illnesses than others – and here we often do make special allowances. The puzzle here concerns which special allowances can be justified.

'Coercion!' alerts us to another important factor concerning sexual equality – and one that can lead to special compensatory allowances. A rhetorical reference is to the 'tame housewife': she has been brainwashed, 'tamed', into preferring to look after the family. It is not what she truly desires. Maybe she is akin to the slave who, brought up in slavery, knows of no better. In some societies, women clearly are not free to realize themselves, being denied proper education, subjected to veils, and much worse. In liberal societies, pressures and customs can still inhibit various free choices. Another puzzle is then: which inhibitions matter? After all, should we be distressed by male bank employees being banned from wearing dresses?

When freedoms are present, if different outcomes persist, why should that lead us to think that something has gone wrong? Some argue that numerical differences between the sexes – more males are company directors, mathematicians, members of parliament – do just show that the freedoms clearly were lacking. Inappropriate nurturing or cultural pressures must be the explanation; and so special arrangements should be made for those who have suffered. But how is it known that such pressures must be the explanation of the differences? Yes, on many occasions – in some countries, on a vast number of occasions – we can spot the coercions, the pressures; but it is an unjustified and curious leap to conclude that when none can be spotted, they must still be lurking somewhere, if numerical differences are present.

A curiosity is the seeming assumption that, were numerical differences to result from what is 'natural' and biological, then they would be acceptable. It is as if it is assumed that nurturing and cultures do not ultimately result from nature; yet, from where else can they result? Further, why is the alleged nature–nurture distinction thought relevant in determining how things *should* be? We often rightly want to interfere with what is natural.

These comments should not blind us to those millions of women, throughout the world, who are treated badly just because they are women. That horrendous fact should not blind us to another: namely, the millions of both women and men who are treated badly because of wars, highly corrupt governments, and uncaring others.

*　　*　　*

Living dangerously, here is Arthur Schopenhauer.

> Women are directly adapted to act as the nurses and educators of our early childhood, for the simple reason that they themselves are childish, foolish, and short-sighted – in a word, are big children all their lives ... Consider how a young girl will toy day after day with a child, dance with it, and sing to it; and then consider what a man, with the very best intentions in the world, could do in her place.

Unsurprisingly, Schopenhauer gets it in the neck from women. Quite what is the evidence he wants us to assess? And what is his reasoning? Rejecting Schopenhauer, though, should not lead us to insist, against all evidence, that typically there are no female–male differences in outlooks and emotions. Genuine free choices of women and men may well generate very different lifestyles, different numbers in occupations – and, in some cases, they seem to do so.

Arguably, the ultimate ideal sought should be that of flourishing lives for all. The call for sexual equality has led to increased awareness of women's differing needs concerning flourishing lives. There is also increasing awareness more generally of the significance of parenthood for many. Parenthood is often promoted through maternity and paternity leave – and promoted in some countries not fearing, well, not obviously fearing, significant population decline. The question then arises whether the special provisions for parenting should take priority over, say, special provision for the childless, male or female. The childless, to flourish, may require careers undamaged through taking long breaks for travel, voluntary work, even champagne drinking. There are different ways of flourishing and different groups, for various reasons, typically secure more opportunities and more flourishing than others. Societies muddle through selecting some groups to promote over others, but which deserve that promotion? Which discriminations are fair? Which equalities are worth seeking? – be they sexual, educational, or even by way of monetary income and outcome regarding quality of life.

Most people accept that at least a reasonable lifespan is a central element in flourishing. Over this, in many countries, men are worse off than women, as, for that matter, are the poor compared with the wealthy. Improving the male lifespan would typically benefit both sexes. So, should resources be diverted to promote sexual equality in that regard? Perhaps the answer is 'yes'. Perhaps, then, men need a lower retirement age than women or extra health care or leisure hours. Should that be a high priority? Should that be up for discussion?

The puzzling heart of sexual equality remains. Which sexual discriminations amount to sexism, to discriminating against one sex without good justification? Which sexual equalities should – and should not – be promoted? After all, there just is a greater demand for female beauticians than male. Does that need to be changed?

30. IF THIS BE JUDGING ...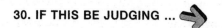

 3. A PILL FOR EVERYTHING?

14. MAN OR SHEEP?

2. ON THE RUN: ALL'S FAIR WITH BEARS?

13

HUMPTY DUMPTY ADVISES MS TURKEY

MS TURKEY: Isn't the world a wonderful place! Fast food delivery service each morning, courtesy of good friend Farmer McDonald; sustained gobbling throughout the day; well-fed night's sleep – up and ready for next morning's delivery at first cock crow.

HUMPTY DUMPTY: Ah, but I have to tell you, Ms T, past farmer performance is no guide to the future.

MS T: How on earth do you know?

HD: Over the years, I've known lots of your relatives. Initially, things go splendidly for them, but … Well, speaking as a friend, let me just say that, were I you, Ms T, I'd quit the farm once December's snows snow, sleigh bells sound, and fairy lights sparkle on fir trees high.

MST *[gulping]*: Thank you, HD – I understand. But you're still relying on past performance as a guide for your kindly advice; yet you said the past was no guide at all.

HD: Your mistake is in thinking that I meant what I said. As I told that silly girl, Alice – she once met me through the looking glass, you know – when I use a word, I make it mean just what I want it to mean.

MST: Isn't that terribly confusing?

HD: Maybe it is; maybe it isn't. It all depends on whether you take past meanings to be a guide to future meanings.

MST: But, but, but …

*   *   *

Let us, for the moment, skate round questions of whether meanings are frozen or fluid. Here is a basic question:

Is the past ever a good guide to the future?

This puzzle is most closely associated with the eighteenth-century philosopher David Hume. Hume was Scottish; but English philosophers sometimes bathe in his glory with Hume as 'British'. Of course, when it comes to John Locke, who was English, well, he is often allowed to remain *English*.

Just because various things have regularly happened it does not follow that they will carry on, regularly so, into the future. Famously, crudely yet rightly, over perhaps centuries, Europeans observed swans – always white swans. From those experiences, they concluded that all swans are white. But, had they nipped to Australia, they could have encountered black swans. From the fact that all observed swans are white, it does not follow that all swans are white. From the fact that I have been breathing for many years, it does not follow that I shall always be breathing.

The puzzle is not solely of what justifies our moving from past cases to future, but what justifies us in moving from some observed cases to the unobserved. At heart, the puzzle rests on the gap between 'some' and 'all' or 'these' and 'those'. It is the problem of induction. Whatever the number of instances of experienced combinations, are we ever justi-fied in expecting similar such combinations, and, if so, why? This is an 'epistemic' question, one concerning knowledge or belief. The underlying metaphysical problem – one of 'what there is in the world' – is: if there are certain regularities, over here, or in the past, are they likely to be repeated over there or in the future?

Sometimes people – even philosophers – cheat. 'That big black bird merely *looks* like a swan. Its feathers are not white, so it's not really a swan.' In that move, we are making 'having white feathers' a necessary condition for being a swan. But if swans are defined as being white, then earlier searches to see whether all swans were white turn out to be pointless. I have told the story before of Mrs Thatcher, when British Prime Minister, announcing that nurses did not go on strike. When striking nurses were pointed out to her, she responded to the effect that, 'Oh, they're not true nurses.'

Accidental associations, white and swan, for example, may well not continue into the future or the spatial elsewhere, but perhaps there are some necessities in nature. Consider: all glass is brittle. Under standard conditions, glass smashes when struck by concrete blocks. We may insist that, if this transparent pane does not smash, then it cannot be glass. Well, all right, let us accept that; but we have merely swept the puzzle to elsewhere. We were wondering whether we could be sure that the next piece of glass we encountered would smash. Now, we know that it will, if – *if* – it really is glass. The new puzzle is: how can we be sure that this transparent material is glass, until we see whether it smashes? Once again, we have to make a leap to what will happen.

* * *

MS T: I see that we ought not to reason from the past being a certain way to the future continuing that way. There's a gap. Perhaps we should just rely on our experience that often things have continued in the same way. The reasoning – inductive reasoning – has typically been successful in the past; so, it is reasonable to expect its continuing success.

HD: Circularity, dear Ms T. How can past successes of inductive reasoning justify future ones?

MS T: Well, I guess we just accept that they do. You continue to balance on that wall, HD – as you know in the past that you can.

HD *[looking nervous]*: Well, sort of ... But, yes, that excellent egg, Hume, made your point. Habit is key. We simply have certain expectations. Perhaps that we have evolved with such expectations is a mark of their reliability.

MS T: That success, though, is only success to date. It may not be success in the future. The human race has expanded over the past, but who knows about the future? Think of current tales of climate warming; yet, who knows? Think of past predictions of global freezes and population explosions.

HD: Point taken, Ms T. But, without reliance on the past, how can we make informed judgements about the future, about fine wall-balancing by eggs such as myself, about tastes of unopened pinot noir wine – and the succulence of the yet to be carved roast turk ... Ooops! Sorry Ms T.

MS T: An easy enough slip, HD. But are we getting confused? Just because past regularities are no guarantee of similar future regularities, may they not offer some likelihood? Is that not reasonable? Mind you, in the investment world, many advertisements proclaim that the past is no guide to the future, yet display fine past performances. Some claim that the past is not *necessarily* a guide.

HD: Yes, even if the past does not have to be a guide – is not necessarily a guide – it may still happen to be one. After all, humans do not have to be so keen on roast potatoes and turkey, yet they ... Sorry, I've put my egg-head in it again.

MS T: My, this is getting to be a habit, HD. I'll soon be eggs-pecting it – on the basis of your past performance. Perhaps we simply need to accept that, in this world, past regularities do happen to be pretty good guides to future ones.

HD: We may even toy with the brilliant thought that the past is necessarily a good guide to the future. If things have been irregular – highly higgledy-piggledy – in the past, that is evidence, though not conclusive evidence, pointing to irregularities in the future.

MS T: I'll need to think on it further ...

HD: I shouldn't hang round, thinking for much longer, Ms T. Whatever we may *think* about the past not properly justifying beliefs about the future, I know, just know, that you should listen out for those farmer footsteps with some trepidation, when those December snows snow. And you'll be right to listen – because of what has happened in the past.

MST: Just as, in view of your past performances, I am justified in believing in your wall-balancing abilities, HD. Musing more, that I understand your words is a tribute to the fact that the past guides us. We cannot even speak or think about these matters without accepting the linguistic past as guide to the future, maybe even necessarily so after all, and ...

[*Crashing sound, as HD falls to the ground.*]

29. HOVE AND LATE: A GRUESOME AFFAIR

17. GOD, CHOCOLATE, AND NEWCOMB: TAKE THE BOX?

27. THE GREATEST MIRACLE?

14

MAN OR SHEEP?

Thomas Hobbes, a key political philosopher of the seventeenth century, wrote that man's life was 'solitary, poor, nasty, brutish, and short'. The obvious reply is, 'It could have been worse, Thomas; it could have been solitary, poor, nasty, brutish – and long.'

Hobbes was describing life before the existence of a state, government, and law. Humans are competitive. They lack reason to trust each other, unless there is a powerful authority that sets laws and punishes law-breakers. In a state of nature, individuals would be in constant conflict or, at least, always on their guard, insecure, and ready for battle. The state of nature, of life pre-government, is a state of war. With the state of nature so horrible, human beings would obviously want to get out, into something better. According to Hobbes, they would come together and agree on a sovereign, an absolute authority, to represent and rule over them, giving them security and opportunity to lead reasonable lives.

There are many puzzles, not least why individuals in the state of nature would risk trusting each other to keep to any agreement. Let us, though, not worry about how government arises. Here we are, living within a state. Let us assume we have a government democratically elected. However, whatever the degree of democracy, laws are imposed that restrict what we may do. We may disapprove of some laws because of some moral or religious principles; we may disapprove of other laws simply because they prevent us from getting what we want. The general concern becomes: by what authority does any government rightfully rule over us?

Why should we obey the state and its laws?

We may answer in practical terms. We obey the law because we are scared of the consequences of disobedience, not wanting to risk fines and imprisonment. The rational thing to do, given the aim of getting on with our lives as best we can, is to obey. When asked whether man or mouse, some of us tend to squeak and take the cheese. Even more so may most of us squeak, when the tentacles of the law and the long arm of the police take hold. We mice may, indeed, be more akin to sheep, sheepishly following each other in our general obedience. Our puzzle though is what, if anything, makes obeying the law the *right* thing to do – even if we could get away with disobeying.

Many of us benefit because of the state's existence: we are defended from others, receive state education, health services, in return for paying taxes. We are better off with law than without. So, we are obligated, in return, to obey the laws that confer those benefits. One immediate objection is that this justification for lawful obedience fails to work for those who overall do not benefit. A significant number do very badly, sleeping rough, being denied state benefits, and being avoided by those better off. Why should they obey? Also, some at society's top may argue that they contribute more than they receive – probably forgetting that they secured the more because of society's stability and protection of gross inequalities often inherited.

Even when overall we do benefit from the state's existence, it does not follow that we are under any obligation to the benefactor. Did we ever sign up, agreeing that we would accept benefits in return for obeying the law? If someone buys us a drink, without our asking, are we under an obligation to buy one in return?

Reference to 'signing up' casts us along another line, a line orientated towards the 'social contract'. What justifies the state and our obedience is that we consented to the set-up. Some philosophers, John Locke and arguably Hobbes, believed that historically some individuals made contracts to be governed by an authority acting in their interests, leading to our societies. Of course, there is no reason to believe in such historical events; but, even if they occurred, whatever relevance do they have for us today? We were not around hundreds of years ago, engaged in any contractual deals.

The response to that last thought is to spot features of our current lives that may indicate consent. We make use of the state's services; we travel freely on the King's highway, notes Locke – well, today the Queen's highway. This shows that we tacitly consent to the state – or does it? Just because we remain in this country, using its facilities, it does not follow that we consent: after all, what other options are available? Can most people afford to go elsewhere? Would other countries, with acceptable laws, permit entry? It is as if we find ourselves on a ship in the middle of the ocean, with the captain making the point that we are free to leave.

*   *   *

Rationality is often wheeled out, to come to the rescue. True, we were not involved in any original social contract; true, our remaining within our society fails to establish consent. But suppose we were rational, not yet in a society, and needing to create society's laws. Suppose, too, we were ignorant of our sex, race, abilities, and the position we probably would reach in society, be it through chance or talent. In such an original position, behind a veil of ignorance, where everything is fair between us, our thinking, even though we remain as individuals, would not be distorted by a distinctive self-interest differing from the self-interest of others. Rather, our common rationality and interests should lead us to see and accept what would be fair laws, benefits, and rights for all. Behind the veil of ignorance, it would seem rational to consent to a society that permitted basic freedoms, did not discriminate between individuals on irrelevant grounds, and provided welfare benefits for when things go badly. After all, behind the veil of ignorance, we have no idea whether we may end up belonging to minority groups or hitting on hard times. If our current society possesses the features it would be rational to consent to behind the veil, then our obedience today is justified by this hypothetical consent, by what is seen as a hypothetical contract.

The response, by way of jibe, is that hypothetical contracts are not worth the paper they are not written upon. Hypothetical consent is not consent. The jibe, though, misses the point. Justifications can rightly involve hypotheticals. Why did you battle with the man, yanking him from the cliff's path, despite his protests? 'Because, had he been sober, he would have consented to the yanking, to save him from risking a fatal fall.'

The resort to the veil of ignorance, to rationality and the hypothetical, though, raises its own puzzles. Quite what does rationality involve behind such a veil? Is it rational, for example, to place liberty higher than greater welfare benefits requiring higher levels of taxation?

Whatever justifications are offered for general obedience to the state, sometimes we morally ought to disobey. Had only many, many consulted their conscience instead of the law, various atrocities, instituted by governments, could have been avoided. Had only many, many been aware of their humanity rather than going along with the mice and the sheep ...

Mind you, that is so easy for me to say and you to read as, in all likelihood, we sit reasonably well off, looking at this book, not having to stand up and be counted – and also not scraping a living in desperate circumstances. We are cocooned, indeed, from millions of dispossessed in the world for whom life is certainly nasty, brutish, and short.

22. VEILS OF WOE: BEATS AND PEEPING TOMS TOO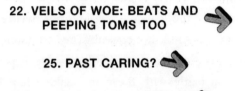

25. PAST CARING?

30. IF THIS BE JUDGING ...

15

... AND THE LIVING IS EASY

Summertime – and, yes, the living is easy, well, easy for some. Our roving reporter is experiencing rural life, interviewing the locals – but what's this? It's bizarre ... She's interviewing a grasshopper and ant.

*　　　*　　　*

What do you do all day, Miss Grasshopper?

'I sing and dance, and dance and sing, across meadows of green, under skies of blue, the sun a-light, a-blazing upon my wing.'

You smile blissfully, Grasshopper, but Ant, I hear you dispute Grasshopper's lifestyle.

'That's right. You should reject it too. The living is easy for this young lady and other grasshoppers – but we workers don't have time for such trivial leisure stuff. We work our socks off day and night – well, we would, if we had socks. Not

for us all the flimsy and fluttering finery of lazy Grasshopper here with her game-playing. We trek out, day after day, food to be gathered, then painstakingly stored for those cold, cold winter days ahead.'

'Hey, no need to rant, dear, dear Ant. Join in with us. Sing and dance, and dance and sing; all your utility is futility, futility. What's the point to your labours, your work, your toils of woe? They're all so, so without point, you know.'

'I'll tell you the point, young lady. You'll come a cropper, believe me. Work is what you have to do to survive. And you listen here: don't you come knocking at my door when you're cold and hungry, freezing in winter's frost – then you'll be sorry. Mark my words!'

'But that's all tomorrow, tomorrow, tomorrow. Think of today – come here, come hither, come play.'

'Frivolity – time wasting. Why am I wasting my time even talking to you? I must get on – must get on.'

Here, I'd better return us to the studio for a time check and traffic news. We mustn't let listeners lapse into grasshopping mode. They have their work to get to, money to earn, bills to pay; but …

Is it better to be the grasshopper?

The Aesop fable alluded to here encourages prudence. If you waste time today, what becomes of you tomorrow? And would Ant be morally obliged to help Grasshopper if she knocks at his door in winter, desperate for food? She would have wittingly allowed herself to slide into winter starvation. Her starvation would have been her own fault. She could have toiled under the summer's sun as Ant did so toil. She brought any winter misfortune upon herself. The fable may, though, generate a puzzle different from that of our moral responsibility for feckless others. This different puzzle asks: what is most valuable in life?

The contrast between Grasshopper and Ant is presented as that between leisure and work, between doing nothing and doing something. Most people, though, readily accept that doing nothing possesses little value. In fact, what exactly is 'doing nothing'? Maybe just lying on a sea-shore, looking into the blue sky, feeling the warmth of the sun; but would that count as the most valuable life? It may be part of a valuable life, but do we not value more, much more?

Grasshopper may be understood as representing those who do things, but who – in contrast to Ant – do not do things that have to be done. Grasshopper plays. Ant toils. Ant toils not because toiling in itself is valuable, but as a necessary means to an end, an end that is valued – namely, being well-fed in winter. Grasshopper plays. In playing, she does something, but the ends of play are neither necessary to achieve nor do they need to be desirable for their own sake. It is the playing that is valuable. Play is typically associated with games; and games, some suggest, are voluntary attempts to overcome unnecessary obstacles.

In work and games we accomplish things, but with games, the goals typically lack value other than being parts of the games. Ant would be much worse off, he thinks, if not well-fed in winter. Pure game-players are not much worse off, if golf balls fail to get holed, footballs never land in goal, and crosswords remain uncompleted. A charm of games can be the utter pointlessness in the ends that are sought. Of course, further ends may be added, such as winning prizes.

The pointlessness of games' ends is matched by the perverse means required to achieve those ends. Players are not allowed to drop golf balls in the holes, carry the football into the net, or look up answers in order to solve the crosswords.

Rules constrain how the goals may be achieved. Games can be good – they can be bad – as games. Good games must be neither very easy, yet nor impossible to complete.

Why value Grasshopper's lifestyle over Ant's toil? Well, Ant's activities are undertaken because of the necessity of the ends. They are undertaken not for their own sake, but for something else. Maybe this detracts from the value of Ant's activities. Play and games lack that external pressure. Of course, Ant triumphs in the end because those hard frosts and snows do come along. But at what cost has he triumphed? What is the value of a life of toil, if one toils only to be well-fed – in order to toil yet again and again? Grasshopper's life, albeit short, has been freed of toiling necessities.

We should, in passing, question whether 'play' captures all that can be valuable, without needing external ends. Paintings and music – creating and appreciating – can be valued in themselves, without any further ends in view.

* * *

People – even philosophers – often favour black or white answers and sharp distinctions. 'Are you journeying to get from A to B? If so, then it would be better to be at B, without the journeying.' Now, on occasions that may be true; but often, when we journey to B, the journeying is also valuable. We should not forget that activities undertaken for a required end may yet also be valued in themselves; and activities valued in themselves may possess the additional value of being the means to something else that is also valuable. How much better, we may imagine, if Grasshopper's game-playing also helped to store food for the winter. How much better if those who – perversely? – delight in peddling gymnasium exercise machines, at the same time generated electricity.

The discussion above raises two further matters.

The first matter is this. Wittgenstein famously pointed to the term 'game' as an example of how we can successfully understand words, even though they lack a certain type of definition. Some think Wittgenstein mistaken; hence the definition of 'game', summarized above, as a voluntary attempt to overcome unnecessary obstacles. However, mountaineering and writing haiku seem to be voluntary attempts to overcome unnecessary obstacles, yet are not usually games; and some necessary work could be nothing but a game for some.

Whether or not Wittgenstein is right about 'game', he is surely right that not all words can be informatively defined by setting out necessary and sufficient conditions for their use. We often need to see how words are used in everyday circumstances rather than seeking formal definitions.

The second 'further matter' is that of identity. Why does Ant in the summer concern himself with how he will be in the winter? Why slave away now, when the future is uncertain – and future fun less likely, as age slows us? More deeply, we have the puzzle of what makes a person today identify herself as being the same person as someone in the past and someone in the future. In my particular case, why do I, Peter Cave, identify with Peter Cave a year ago or twenty years ago, and Peter Cave a year into the future, when my desires and beliefs and character may have radically altered?

Returning to Ant, why does that future ant, as we may view Ant in the future, have a hold over him now, in the summer? 'Because it will still be *me*,' he replies. But will it? Is that again too much 'black or white'?

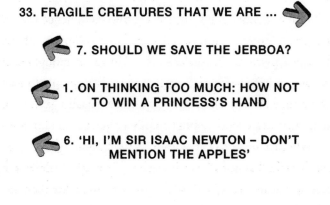

33. FRAGILE CREATURES THAT WE ARE ...

7. SHOULD WE SAVE THE JERBOA?

1. ON THINKING TOO MUCH: HOW NOT TO WIN A PRINCESS'S HAND

6. 'HI, I'M SIR ISAAC NEWTON – DON'T MENTION THE APPLES'

16

'MY BELOVED IS MINE' *or* 'THE TROUBLE WITH FOOTBALL IS THE OTHER TEAM'

Lovers are likened to the mad, the mad with seething brains – and not merely because lovers kiss, bite, and whisper intimate childish names. What lovers see in their beloved, the world often sees not at all. And that seems like a madness.

Lucy finds her man, Lenny, exciting and handsome, everything for which she longed. In Lucy's eyes, Lenny lives on the edge, has unusual thoughts – and, as for his ravishing smile, well … The world, though, sees Lenny as no good, a layabout, a little lopsided in the lips' department. Ottone gazes at Poppea: she is charming, beautiful, coquettish, yet bountiful. The world spots Poppea as manipulative, scheming, and a bit overweight.

Lovers do not see what the world sees. 'Love looks not with the eyes, but with the mind.' Cupid is pictured blind, blind to rules and restraint. Of course, in quick response, we may reflect that love can reveal more than the world first sees: the love of a good woman, or man, may work wonders on those so beloved.

Lovers, of course, often lust for each other. There is the urge to kiss, embrace, and much more; and, as the above portrays, lovers possess tendencies to project perfections. They may place each other on pedestals which, as the quip goes, have little scope for manoeuvre and considerable scope for falls. Imperfections may receive positive renderings. Lenny's lopsided smile is distinctively sweet to Lucy; and Poppea's slight weight problem is, for Ottone, an abundance to love. When things go well, misperceptions and renderings are mutually for the better.

Why does Ottone not spot Poppea's scheming nature? 'Ah, that's because he's in love.' The love is offered as explanation of Ottone's over – or under – sight; it explains why he finds the weight appealing. Yet, why does Ottone love Poppea? 'Ah, that is because he sees her as such a beautiful, bountiful woman.' This two-way explanation is no true explanation at all, for it loops round: the positive rendering is explained by the love; yet the love is explained by the positive rendering.

Explaining lovers' perceptions forms one puzzle. Maybe the solution needs recognition of the role of time: love develops. A particular feature of Poppea sparks desire in Ottone and, if things go well, other features come to the fore, seen in the light of developing desire. Things spiral and grow – and features become embellished and enhanced, intensifying the flushes and fervour. Desires fan out, turning to a more embracing love. Whatever best explains the spiral and other changes, another puzzle remains: what is it that lovers yearn and lust after, when they speak of wanting each other?

What do lovers desire?

What brings desires to an end may not be what is desired. You may desire a holiday, yet the desire is quelled by an emergency intervening, the holiday forgotten. You yearn for another drink, but the sight of a drunk brings a halt to that yearning: you no longer feel like a drink at all. The emergency and the sight of the drunk brought the desires to an end, but the emergency and the sight were not the objects of those desires.

Consider two lovers lusting after each other. People tend to believe that, because orgasm typically brings an end to immediate lusts, it is the orgasmic end that the lovers really desire. Yet, with the holiday and drink examples in mind, that may be a mistaken belief.

When the lusting is also a loving, what, indeed, is desired? Lovers, metaphorically, devour each other with their eyes, wanting to possess each other – but what is going on?

There may be no simple answer. Certainly, lovers take pleasure in each other, in each other's body, thought, and personality; but pleasurable sensations are not the sole end. Were pleasurable sensations all that mattered, a sensation-generating machine would do just as well; but few people love and lust after machines – and machines lust not at all.

Lovers, as with friends, may value simply walking quietly through a glade, hand in hand, eating together, and sharing music. They are doing something together, but not merely in that they are each taking part in the same activity. Rather, there is a 'we'; *we* are walking along the seashore. *We* are at a party – even though in different corners of the room. Two people may play chess together, yet not in the loving sense just proffered – for the players may be held together solely by the chess. Two (or more) lovers or friends, though, may play and delight – just as they may dance and sing – as one. And, when it is love and not mere friendship, the 'we' involves, of course, intimacies of body.

Pleasures in love – and friendships – also require reciprocation. Lenny's pleasure in Lucy typically heightens Lucy's pleasure in Lenny which heightens Lenny's pleasure – and so on. However far we may spiral – presumably the limit falls well below 'the sky's the limit' – its familiarity reminds us that love is between people, people who can delight in the other's delight. That is one reason why the lonely night-time cuddles of the pillow fail to transform that pillow into a substitute lover.

Love typically involves at least *two* people, not one – yet that too creates puzzle. Lovers want more than pillows, yet when lovers speak of 'we', they endanger the individual, the individual being swallowed. We sometimes hear cries, 'Give me space; let me be *me*.' The stronger may devour or overwhelm the weaker, the cries silenced, yet the stronger, the dominant, is now alone, unloved, and unloving. How much more so would our human selves be lost, were we to engage in the ecstatic love of a being as dominant as God – for that is an unequal relationship indeed. That relationship would certainly endanger our individuality. Maybe that is why certain religious believers and mystics, when anticipating eternal survival through God, do not anticipate personal survival at all. They will be lost in the One.

* * *

Images of love often display the body as territory. John Donne writes:

> Licence my roving hands, and let them go,
> Before, behind, between, above, below.
> O my America! My new-found-land ...

Jean-Paul Sartre, the French intellectual of the twentieth century, goes pessimistically and metaphysically further. Sexual desire is intrinsically unstable and, in some way, contradictory. In desiring the other, we seek to turn that person into a thing, into flesh, while still wanting that other to be a free agent, loving us.

'I want all of you' we, as lovers, might say; but how can we possess the person, the beloved, with his or her subjective gaze upon the world? Sartre hence quips, 'The trouble with football is the other team.' Yet, with a paradoxical 'of course', the other team is essential to the game and to love.

Plato offers a different picture, a picture of lovers seeking their other halves, perhaps resulting in a mutual unified transformation, the original whole found, with both individuals then lost within that whole.

And so it is that different approaches to love paint love as, in one way or another, endangering individuality – either through conquering the other or losing the self.

Images of love also involve mysterious flights. 'My beloved is mine, and I am his: he feedeth among the lilies,' sings the *Song of Solomon*. 'Behold, thou art fair, my love; behold, thou art fair; thou hast doves' eyes within thy locks: thy hair is as a flock of goats that appear from Mount Gilead.'

Love puzzles. With a Sartrean sense, well before Sartre, John Dryden speaks of lovers:

> They gripe, they squeeze, their humid tongues they dart,
> As each would force their way to t'other's heart,
> In vain; they only cruise about the coast,
> For bodies cannot pierce, nor be in bodies lost,
> As sure they strive to be ...

Love puzzles, yet matters to us all. That it matters creates more puzzlement. When in love, love has huge significance, even though we may be able to step back and recognize its absurdity. With that absurdity in mind, although we are probably unaware of Lord Chesterfield's name, his famous quip may yet spring to the fore.

'In the act of love, the pleasure is momentary, the position ridiculous and the expense damnable.'

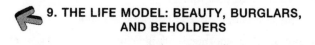

9. THE LIFE MODEL: BEAUTY, BURGLARS, AND BEHOLDERS

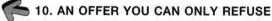

10. AN OFFER YOU CAN ONLY REFUSE

19. WHAT'S WRONG WITH EATING PEOPLE? *or even* **WHO'S FOR DINNER?**

33. FRAGILE CREATURES THAT WE ARE ...

17

GOD, CHOCOLATE, AND NEWCOMB:
TAKE THE BOX?

A paradox seemingly miles away from God and chocolate has fascinated philosophers for the last forty years; it is Newcomb's. Before we connect it with the everyday, here comes the paradox.

A mind-reader seems able to read minds. You are presented with two boxes. In one, £10,000 is clearly in view. The other, the surprise box, is closed, its contents concealed. What you know is that the mind-reader, after reading your mind, will either have popped £1 million or nothing at all into the surprise box. So, in front of you there are two boxes: one with £10,000 clearly visible; another, the closed surprise box, with either zero or £1 million already there.

You are given the following choice. You may take either both boxes or just the surprise. Thousands of people have been given the choice. Those who have taken both have always found the surprise box empty; they have always ended up

with just the £10,000. People who have taken only the surprise box have happily found the £1 million within.

People speculate. Maybe the mind-reader assesses people's characters. If she judges that players are not hugely greedy, settling for the surprise box alone, she rewards them accordingly by popping the £1 million into that box. If she judges players to be greedy, wanting as much as possible, likely to grab both boxes, she leaves the surprise box empty. To date, she has always been right. Who knows how she does it – but she does. It is known that it is possible for her to make mistakes, but she has not made one yet.

You want to get the most money you can. You do not want to risk losing the £1 million; yet you do not want to end up with nothing. The £10,000 is certainly worth having, but winning the £1 million is better still – and getting both the £10,000 and the £1 million would be best. What is it rational to do?

Which way are you jumping? Try it on friends.

Should you open both boxes or solely the surprise box?

Many philosophers follow the 'already there' approach:

> Look, either the surprise box already contains the £1 million or it's already empty. If it's already empty, then obviously I should take both boxes – in order to get the £10,000. If the surprise box already contains the £1 million, then I should also take both boxes, securing both the £1 million and the £10,000. There can be no dispute. Any rational person – and I, being a philosopher – must take both boxes.

The retort is the 'evidential' approach:

> Consider the evidence. Whenever people have taken both boxes, the surprise box is empty. Who knows how the mind-reader works it out, but somehow she does. Obviously, the rational thing to do, given the evidence, is to take just the surprise box. Only by my doing that will I secure the £1 million. All I can say about your 'already there' reasoning is: if it's so very clever, how come people who reason as you do aren't rich?

We may reel with the reasoning, between the 'already there' and 'evidential' approaches.

Perhaps, we decide to take the surprise box only; but then reason's teeny voice whispers that the mind-reader will therefore have already filled the surprise box with the £1 million, given the way we have decided. Hence, we may as well take both boxes after all, the 'already there' approach coming to the fore. But now we reflect that the mind-reader, being so clever, would have judged that we would take that next step in the reasoning, switching to favouring both boxes; so, it would be better after all to remain faithful to the original decision to take the surprise box only ... But, the 'already there' reasoning cuts in again. And so on ... The reasoning loops round.

My approach questions the puzzle's casual beginning. How is the mind-reader so successful? At least, how could she be successful when dealing with rational players? As we have seen, rational philosophers reach opposing or unstable conclusions about what to do. Of course, so-called rational philosophers – heaven forbid? – may end up defending one line of reasoning over another because of their psychological tendencies: risk-takers or greedy, overawed by evidence or cautious, committed to one type of philosophical theory or another. And we can seek to explain other reasoners' choices also on the basis of their psychological tendencies. Paradoxically, though, when assessing what it is *rational* for me to do, I cannot see my own decisions as the results of such tendencies.

The mind-reader, though, is back in business, if decisions, even of so-called rational players, result from players' psychological tendencies; but if they result purely from what it is rational to do – well, players and mind-reader are at sea. Our mind-reader would indeed be a phantasy – though the underlying puzzle is not, in that we now have a deep puzzle of how psychology and biology connect with rational and logical reasoning.

*   *   *

Whatever happened to God and genetics? Some godly believers, when tragedy has struck, pray or make sacrifices to their God, hoping that, for example, their daughter was not killed in a recent disaster. Maybe they reason that, through prayer or sacrifice, their daughter will have been saved, God having foreseen their actions, their pleas and sacrifices. This is akin to the evidential approach: take the surprise box only; sacrifice the definite £10,000. Some believers, however, may reason that their daughter is already saved or not; so why lose time or money through prayer or sacrifice? This is the 'already there' approach.

Some religious believers hold that it is predestined whether they gain eternal bliss or not – yet they still judge it important to lead godly lives to secure that eternal bliss. In that case, they are rejecting the 'already there' approach and following the evidential approach.

Turning to genetics, suppose there is a correlation

between certain genes and proneness to heart disease. Perhaps people so prone also eat lots of chocolate. Therefore, perhaps we should give up our chocolate consumption, hoping that we are thereby unlikely to have the undesirable genetic factor. In such reasoning, we are, so to speak, foregoing the chocolate box, the £10,000 box, in the hope that genetically our surprise box is filled with health. Here, this is a highly dubious argument. It would be better to argue that the genetic factor is indeed already fixed; so, if the factor is the cause of the proneness, we may as well have the chocolate and hope – maybe against hope – that the surprise box is yet filled with health. Of course, it may be that the genetic factor causes the chocolate desire, but it is the chocolate that actually causes the disease proneness; then, it could be rational to try to resist the chocolates.

These puzzles arise because we are uncertain which are causal factors, which irrelevant side-effects, and which accidental correlations. We often lack understanding of how nature works. The Newcomb paradox baffles because we lack understanding of how the mind-reader works.

Newcomb's weirdness is shown by embellishing the tale, making the surprise box also open to view, with players seeing whether the £1 million is present. We then add to the story: yet, even when the £1 million is present and on view, players take only that box instead of taking both. This highlights the tale's mystery – a mystery present in Newcomb from the very beginning.

Genetic research seeks to eradicate mystery, distinguishing causes from coincidences, but we still live with one central mystery, namely, how causes relate to free choices and reasoning. Richard Dawkins of *The Selfish Gene* fame seems to find room for freedom through 'our brains rebelling against our genes'; but whatever does that mean and how does it provide room for free choices? How causes relate to free choices and, indeed, reasoning, is the deep mystery lurking within Newcomb's paradox, and indeed with our succumbing to chocolate, yet doing so freely. Or not so freely …

 1. ON THINKING TOO MUCH: HOW NOT TO WIN A PRINCESS'S HAND

 11. SLOTHFUL SLOTH SPEAKS: 'WHAT WILL BE, WILL BE'

10. AN OFFER YOU CAN ONLY REFUSE

18

THE BRAIN

I've recently lost my appetite. That's unsurprising, I suppose, given that I'm just a brain in a vat – well, so they tell me. In fact, I reside in a precious Grecian vase, size large, and not just any old vat. At first I thought they were making fun of me, but then my experiences started to go haywire. Sometimes they cut out completely and I just experience a blank. They tell me not to worry. I'm in good hands. They promise to let me see me one day, but currently they feed me experiences as if I were at home, gazing through the window, feeding the pigeons – or out dancing and prancing, drinking champagne with young men of my dreams. Ah, that's the life.

Of course, I do worry. I sometimes dwell on my vase-free days, when I was more than just a brain. But that way of look-ing at things is mistaken – so they insist. I've always just been a brain – but now I am a brain in a vase and not a brain in a typical human body. 'Typical' did they say? I'll have them know that mine was highly desired and desirable, more so than any Grecian vase, however precious.

I guess we all knew that things like this could happen. Years ago, when my arm was chopped off, I continued to have experiences as if I had an arm, despite being armless. I experienced what is called a 'phantom limb'. Technology was developing fast, and I soon had an impulse machine plugged into my nervous system. By tinkering with the machine's settings, I could give myself experiences as if the missing arm, the phantom limb, were in the right place, even as if it were holding a book. With my body's deterioration — more bits falling off — neurologists thought it best to concentrate on preserving my brain. That is how I, brain, ended up in a vase — antique, let me remind you. I undergo experiences — they seem real enough — which the neurologists judge to cohere with my former life. The experiences result from their stimulating my brain's cells.

So, here I am. Well, I am not sure what that means these days. I am here in the vase, but my experiences are, as I said, mainly as if I am carrying on normally. And I do have a say in what happens. They can tell from the neural activities how my vocal chords would then be moving, if I had any, to express what I am thinking and wanting.

News has, though, just come in of an incident. My brain was accidentally sliced in the night, right down the middle. Apparently, that's no problem. They had contingency plans. The neurological changes transmitted from one hemisphere to another continue — this time by some wireless transmitters attached to each hemisphere. They have sorted out the right speed of transmission. Mind you, I am feeling queasy. What if such accidents happen again – and again ... ?

Can a brain have experiences?

Many believe that we essentially are our brains. Hearts, livers, and lungs can be transplanted; arms and legs can be chopped off. What is responsible for my continuing to have my experiences is my brain. Science fiction and horror stories of the 'brain in vat' ilk abound. As philosophers, we are concerned with whether the idea even makes sense.

Some cells in the brain die, but the millions that remain end up, through nutrition, having their molecules, atoms, and electrons changed over time. The particular brain stuff is not important to our identity; what seems key is the configuration of electrical activity, properties, and chemical levels. Let us sum this up: experiences depend upon various neurological changes occurring in certain sequences. If that is true, then why should it matter whether the brain is kept as one unit, or sliced – as happened to poor Biv, 'Brain in Vase', as we may call her? All that matters seems simply to be the right configuration of billions of neurological changes of the right type. How the individual changes are brought about is irrelevant – so long as they are brought about. After all, particular changes do not have impressed upon them how they have been caused.

The above line of thought brings trouble. To see how, let us reduce the billions of neurological changes a little – well, radically – down to three changes, A, B, and C, that are of the right configuration, intensity, and so on, for Biv to have a certain experience. We can rebuild the complexity by multiplying what is said about A, B, and C billions of times.

A particular experience results from A being followed by B being followed by C. If we think of A, B, C being of certain types, then perhaps that type of experience for Biv results from an A-type change being followed by a B-type and then a C-type. That event A causes B and B then causes C does not seem essential to the story, but just that A, B, and C occur in the right sequence. Of course, usually such events occur inside a single human body. For Biv, though, such events now occur in a vase; but, in theory, it seems, A could have been in America, B in Britain, and C in China. So long as the neurological features are of the right type, manifested at the right time, then the relevant experience should occur for Biv. Any A-type change cannot tell, so to speak, how close a B-type is – and so on. Thinking more, is the time sequence even important? After all, A, B, and C do not register the existence of each other as being before or after.

We could take further puzzling steps. Given the billions of neurological changes happening in each human being and the billions of human beings, do we need even to contrive the special existence of A, B, and C? Will not changes of those types be occurring in the skulls of populations in any case, maybe A in American Angela's brain, B in British Bernie's, and C in Chinese Chou's? If that is so, then our Biv is undergoing experiences without the need to retain even her brain, however much broken and dispersed. Indeed, a whole mishmash of experiences must be occurring for a vast number of unknown people with neither bodies nor brains. What an incredible and crazy thought.

Modesty and humility – well, the conclusion's bizarre features – suggest that the reasoning is radically faulty. One obvious thought is that, for experiences, we need the body after all; but that alone does not save us from weird results. We could imagine a brainless human body linked in the right way, by wireless, to neurological changes such as our A, B, and C thousands of miles away. That body would then be moved by the wireless transmissions, as if a brain undergoing those changes were present within it. Does a person with experiences result?

See the depths and intrigues of philosophical reasoning – and the dangers when philosophers fear not the darkness lurking within those depths.

* * *

The error would seem to be the casual separation of a human being, a person, into parts. Yes, we can amputate limbs, and engage in organ transplants, while retaining the same person. However, it does not follow that a brain in a vase would have experiences, even if the brain were undergoing the same internal changes that, when properly humanly embodied, would have ensured experiences for a person.

We confront bizarre puzzles, even without 'brain in vase' tales. Consider some of your current experiences, of the sight of chairs, the taste of coffee, the sounds of rustling papers. Experiences of the same type and configuration, it seems, could well be occurring elsewhere. If they are distinct experiences of the same type, what makes them someone else's rather than yours? What makes *your* experiences yours?

Perhaps when two people have the same thought, there really is just one thought, one thought shared by two people. That approach, even if right for thoughts, would seem simply wrong, if applied to pains. My pain, however similar to yours, is still the one that I experience and you do not. But could human biology have been differently constituted? Might human biology have been such that you, for example, could experience headaches located in the Queen's head – and the Queen also experience those very aches? Consider Siamese twins, joined at the hip. They could both experience the 'same' pain at the join, but, however similar, must there be two distinct pains?

The answer is probably 'yes'. A pain is not logically separable from the individual experiencing the pain. It seems impossible that my experiencing the pain in the Queen's head could be identical with the Queen's experiencing.

Mind and body – psychological and physical states – are

intermingled; and, when we seek to untangle, we hit perplexities. Letters of the alphabet scattered around the universe do not make words and sentences. Neurological changes, similarly scattered, do not make a person's experiences. With some matters of mind, what matters, it seems, is as property owners say: location, location, location.

26. BEAUTY AWAKE

6. 'HI, I'M SIR ISAAC NEWTON – DON'T MENTION THE APPLES'

3. A PILL FOR EVERYTHING?

4. IN NO TIME AT ALL

19

WHAT'S WRONG WITH EATING PEOPLE?
or even WHO'S FOR DINNER?

'I could eat you,' she said, she with the sparkling white teeth and devouring eyes, her arms flung round my neck. How could I not be flattered, receiving such warm and welcoming attention, in the club that had just so eagerly admitted me as member?

'Who's for dinner?' some others asked. Well, I was hungry; and present were bright and beaming people – generous to boot, for no membership fee had been demanded. I was an honorary fellow, they said. Naive little me – little did I realize that my enthusiastic 'yes' to dinner would lead me to the cooking pot, not as guest diner or even guest chef, but – *gulp* – as guest 'about to be dined upon'. These people were generous sure enough, but generous to a fault, as I was soon to discover.

Serve Man was the club's motto – and it slowly dawned on me what this meant. Yes, cannibalism was alive and well in

London's Pall Mall. It looked as if, while I should soon be dead, I should not be much buried – just stewed, with, I trusted, at least a fine garnish.

*   *   *

We may deal quickly with the scenario sketched, once we have the background question: what's wrong with eating people? After all, I had not consented to their gastronomic intentions and was far from wanting to be cooked; so, that was why eating me was wrong.

Jonathan Swift gave satirical voice to eating babies and the young, to stave off impending starvation. The idea has not been much taken up. True, in extreme cases when, for example, survivors of air crashes would otherwise die, people typically accept that eating those already deceased is morally permissible. Many people, though, would be appalled at the dining habits of our club above, even if members ate only humans recently deceased through natural cause or accident. Yet, many of these appalled people are probably pleased to be blood donors, when alive, and pleased to donate organs on death.

To maintain focus, we cast to one side cases when eating those accidentally or naturally deceased is required because of imminent starvation. Those instances excepted, is something otherwise wrong with the consumption of human remains by humans, even when such cannibalism is voluntarily agreed? After all, many of us enthusiastically eat the flesh of other creatures – fish, fowl, and beasts of the field – and sometimes we savour, sometimes unwittingly, snakes, whales, and crocodiles, even the odd cat, dog, and chimp. Yet only the perverted would defend eating people – it seems.

Whatever is wrong with eating people?

Many creatures – cows, sheep, pigs – would not have existed, but for our husbandry; yet does that give us the right to kill and eat them? Were it to do so, we could return to Swift's proposal and defend farming human babies. The argument is, of course, bad. Just because we created the individuals, we do not possess rights to destroy them – certainly not, if the created possess interests of their own, as arguably animals and babies do. Even a Picasso who creates a great painting, appreciated by millions, may be wrong to destroy his creation.

Many of us, of course, seek to justify the painless killing of non-human animals for food. Maybe a super-species would farm humans, arguing that we humans, a lesser species, suffered little loss, if painlessly killed. That would justify eating people – though not by people. The 'super-species thought' may rightly encourage us not to be so casual in our meat-eating ways.

One man's meat may be another man's person, and there are standard, pragmatic arguments against people-pies, *homo sapiens bleu*, and tinned man or woman.

Were the eating of people to be accepted simply as a pleasurable dish – or maybe not so pleasurable – then, it may be said, we should be devaluing human life in general. Even if such eating were permitted only of those who died naturally or by accident – carrying 'donate for eating' cards – our way of looking at each other could alter for the worse. The looking would be affected by the cooking. After all, some argue that some pornography encourages men to view women as flesh, devaluing their personhood. With person cooking accepted, maybe we would regard others as lumps of flesh, commodities, rather than persons. But is this likely? Just because we would be treating corpses in one way, why should we slip into a related attitude to living people?

Respect for persons involves respect for their bodies –

and such respect extends to a person's corpse. Having human corpses, hanging in butcher shops, or tinned man or woman available on supermarket shelves, merely to provide dining variety, undermines the respect. It certainly differs from using organs of the deceased to save others' lives.

Consider households that keep a few turkeys – Lucinder, Ludwig, and Ludmilla – with the intention of fattening them for Christmas. When Christmas comes, not many in the family enjoy tucking into Lucinder and the others. The names have helped to make the turkeys honorary members of our human community.

We de-humanize people, block out respect, reducing their status to mere bundles of flesh, by addressing them, even when face to face, simply by numbers – as done in concentration camps. De-humanization dangers are even present when, for example, patients are known simply as the 'appendix' or 'hernia'. Yet, there are cases and cases. Cases vary, depending on context, intentions, and perceptions. People sometimes may rightly be treated as just bodies. Stelarc, an artist, has engaged in street suspension, piercing his body with hooks, hanging his body over New York City. Was he degrading himself? It is not clear that he was; he remained a voluntary agent in that use of his body as apparently artistic object.

We have pictured human corpses dangling in butcher shops; and such scenes would deeply offend. Yet have we really shown anything to be morally wrong with people wishing to be eaten after their natural death – and those wishes being respected, given suitable regulation and discretion? We have a natural repugnance at the idea, but is there anything immoral?

*   *   *

Respect may be shown in diverse ways. Consider a society where people may choose how their lives and remains should end. Just as today we respect people's wishes whether to be cremated or buried – and even accept that a few mothers after birth cook the placentas – so, in that society, a choice could be made to be eaten. Perhaps a highly significant and ritualistic dining ceremony exists, with only the deceased's loved ones present. Perhaps the ritual is symbolic of ultimate or eternal bonding, of 'connecting' with the deceased. In such a society, people would feel their lives ended badly if the appropriate ceremonies failed to take place. The dining may be associated with a sense of religious oneness or of the flesh metaphorically sustaining the living. Some could see the eating more as worthy sacrificing to the gods. Others may regard life as a work of art, requiring the right ending, just as do novels and music.

Such rituals, with the justifications offered, would today generate laughter or disgust; they would not be taken in the right spirit. It does not follow, though, that there is anything morally wrong in the proposed society. Let us hasten to add: this is not a slide into moral relativism. It is not a slide at all, for, in justifying the dining practices, we deploy values readily recognized across cultures: respecting people's wishes, connecting with others, manifesting love. It does, though, remind us that respecting people can take different forms.

Eating people could be a significant practice in a highly moral world. E. M. Forster's injunction 'only connect' — empathizing, bonding, valuing other people's wishes — may now come to mind. It may come to mind with the addition of a more literal rendering than intended. People who, in the circumstances just outlined, value eating people and being eaten are indeed valuing Forster's injunction.

'Only connect.'

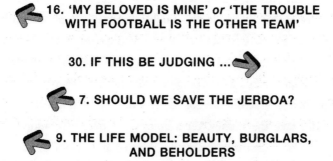

16. 'MY BELOVED IS MINE' *or* **'THE TROUBLE WITH FOOTBALL IS THE OTHER TEAM'**

30. IF THIS BE JUDGING ...

7. SHOULD WE SAVE THE JERBOA?

9. THE LIFE MODEL: BEAUTY, BURGLARS, AND BEHOLDERS

20

HOW TO GAIN WHATEVER YOU WANT

An eminent British philosopher gave a lecture in the United States about fifty years ago. The lecturer was J. L. Austin – John Langshaw Austin – a master of the nuance, and grammatical felicity and infelicity in the English language, a philosopher whose writings consisted of finer and finer linguistic distinctions. In his lecture, Austin made the point that an interesting fact about the English language is that a double negation makes a positive – if he did not *not* take the money, then it looks as if he did take the money. Yet a double positive, 'yes' added to 'yes', does not make a negative. Immediately from the audience came forth the sceptical mutter, 'Yeah, yeah.'

With the above background, consider the following two puzzles, seemingly of impeccable reasoning. Allow me to orientate one in which you lose; the other in which you win. You could, of course, always be the winning participant – or the loser.

Here is a 'lose everything' puzzle. A woman, sitting at a bar, offers you the following deal, wanting to know if you are happy with its conditions.

Accept this offer of a holiday in Venice – you can take some-one with you – and all you have to do is pay me £10; every-thing else is free. There are no strings about the holiday: return first-class tickets, first-class hotel, and so on. Here is one further condition. If what I say next is true, then I keep the £10 and you have the holiday at no further cost; if what I say next is false, then you must accept the £10 back, but still have the holiday free.

How can you lose? There are no snags about the holiday. You would like to go to Venice, see the art – and so forth. Either way, you are surely bound to have the splendid Venetian break. At worst, it costs you a mere £10. And you may even have the £10 returned. Rational man that you are, you eagerly accept. She takes the £10, with a coy smile; and then says:

Either I shall return the £10 or you will pay me £1 million.

Before we examine what has gone wrong, here is a 'win everything' similar puzzle. Find someone – say, Melissa – with some valuable item that you crave. Maybe you want her fine yacht. You ask her:

Q1. Will you give the same answer, 'yes' or 'no', to this question as to the next?

Melissa hesitates. She has no idea what you are going to ask, so it would be foolish to commit either way. You reassure her, saying that you are happy for her to decide which way to answer *after* you have asked the second question; but would she merely agree that she will answer truthfully 'yes' or 'no'. If she still hesitates, slip her some fivers to agree – after all, it is easy money: she is free to answer either 'yes' or 'no'. She agrees. You now ask her:

Q2. Will you give me your yacht?

She may immediately answer 'no'; but can she give that answer truthfully? After all, how is she going to answer that first question now? Logic can indeed puzzle us.

How have you lost a million, yet gained a yacht?

We tackle the 'yacht' tale first. Melissa has agreed to answer the first question 'yes' or 'no'. If she answers 'yes', that commits her to the same answer, 'yes', to the question about giving you the yacht. 'Yes' to *the same* keeps us with 'yes'. If she answers 'no' to the first question, that commits her to not answering the same to the yacht question, hence also making a 'yes'. 'No' to *the same* switches us to 'yes'. The offer, of 'yes' or 'no' answers, appeared to be leaving her with alternatives, but it did not. 'No' repeated is 'no' to 'no', that is 'yes'. 'Yes' repeated – 'yes' to 'yes' – also delivers 'yes'. Of course, maybe saying 'yeah, yeah' sceptically as a response could leave us baffled as to whether it is a 'yes' or a 'no' – but that was not an option.

How about the £1 million puzzle? She says, 'Either I shall return the £10 or you will pay me £1 million.' Suppose what she says is false: for it to be false, just considering what she says, she must not return the £10. But conditions are that she does return the £10, if it is false; hence, there is a contradiction, whether or not you pay the £1 million. So, what she says cannot be false. Therefore, what she says must be true. But if it is true, then that must be because either she returns the £10 or you pay her the £1 million. It cannot be because she returns the £10; the conditions state that she keeps the £10, if what she says is true in her statement. Hence it can only be true because you pay her the £1 million. So, you are £1 million down. Once again, conditions have been rigged to ensure a 'yes', an affirmative, a 'true', to what is wanted.

*   *   *

Lurking in many paradoxes are presuppositions deserving challenge. A dangerous presupposition is that having to answer 'yes' or 'no', or 'true' or 'false', is a fair request. In a classic case, the police ask the suspect, 'Have you stopped beating your wife? Yes or no.' Answering 'yes' implies that you indeed used to, although you are now reformed. Answering 'no' implies that you did – and tells us that, bad character that you are, you continue to beat her. The suspect was afforded no opportunity to challenge the presupposition.

He was not first asked, 'Did you beat your wife?' Then, only if he answered 'yes' should he have been asked, 'Do you still?'

We should be wary of 'yes or no' demands, of surprising offers however attractive they may seem. When contemplating matters abstractly, that is easy to say; but when confronted by tempting offers down here on Earth, well, we can be easily seduced into giving them a clearly affirmative 'yes, yes', instead of being rightly sceptical with the 'yeah, yeah'.

24. THE UNOBTAINABLE: WHEN 'YES' MEANS 'NO'

 8. WHEN ONE MAKES TWO: DRESSING UP

 1. ON THINKING TOO MUCH: HOW NOT TO WIN A PRINCESS'S HAND

11. SLOTHFUL SLOTH SPEAKS: 'WHAT WILL BE, WILL BE'

21

'I AM THE GREATEST' *or* 'THERE AIN'T NO SANITY CLAUS'

G: I am the greatest.

I: The greatest what?

G: The greatest being.

I: Ah, you mean *God*.

G: That's right – or *Allah* or *Yahweh*. Names don't hurt me, whatever people say. I am, after all, the greatest – the greatest being than which nothing greater can be conceived, dreamt of, imagined.

I: So I hear, but you don't exist.

G: You're talking to me.

I: I talk to myself.

G: That's true – and even true now. Being the greatest being I have no need for chat. This is a dialogue with yourself; yet, if you reason correctly, you'll realize that I must exist – and not just in your mind, imagination or dreams.

I: How come?

G: Look, you agree that my existence is not straightaway ruled out. You can make sense of my existing.

I: I'm not sure, once I start thinking about it. But let's suppose that I can – that there can be a being that is all powerful, all knowing, even all perfect, that created the universe. However, that said, there's simply no evidence for you, O greatest conceivable one.

G: That's true. Despite what many believe, I left no signs in the world. Don't focus on the universe. Don't even focus on your self. Focus on the very thought of me.

I: Okay, I have the idea of the greatest conceivable being – I think.

G: Indeed, that being than which nothing greater can be conceived – excellent. Now, suppose that I do not exist.

I: I don't need to suppose. You don't.

G: Let's pretend that is true. Then, were I to exist, it seems that I should be greater than the greatest conceivable being, according to your idea of the greatest conceivable being.

I: Ah, a contradiction.

G: Well, only a contradiction if your idea is really of a being that both lacks existence and is the greatest conceivable being – for such a non-existent being could not be the greatest conceivable being. How could such a being be the greatest, with such a glaringly obvious defect as non-existence? Perhaps you now grasp that I exist.

Must God, Allah, Yahweh, the greatest conceivable being, exist?

Our little dialogue is a version of the ontological argument put forward by the eleventh-century St Anselm of Canterbury. Such ontological arguments, in one form or another, have received considerable support, yet also considerable rejection – and recently, mainly rejection. Major philosophers have lined up – some for; some against. Descartes for; Hume against. Leibniz for; Kant against.

One challenge is: how can any reflections, based solely on the meanings of words, on which ideas we possess, lead to conclusions about reality? We have ideas of unicorns, mermaids, and Santa Claus, yet we need to search the world to establish whether such items exist.

Should we be impressed by that challenge? After all, from analysing our ideas, we conclude that certain things can *not* exist in reality. Once we grasp the nature of squares and circles, we conclude that there are no square circles. Furthermore, once we understand the number series, we can conclude that a prime number *must* exist between seventeen and twenty-three. Of course, these examples are distinctive: they concern abstract entities, entities that we, in any case, cannot experience through the senses or gain evidence for via scientific investigations. We may, though, also show, by reasoning alone, that certain hypothesized everyday empirical entities cannot exist – for example, a creature that at the same time is both capable and incapable of flight.

Some suggest that ontological arguments muddle the idea of X with X. Our idea of an elephant is of a creature with a trunk, but the idea does not itself sport a trunk. The arguments' seeming force, the suggestion runs, rests upon a threatened contradiction, resulting from such a muddle. We see this, when we present a key stage in some of the arguments.

If we suppose that the greatest conceivable being fails to exist, then, were he to exist, he would be greater than the greatest conceivable being – but that is a contradiction.

The mistake here lies in treating our idea of the greatest conceivable being as itself a contender for such greatness. Yes, were the greatest conceivable being to exist, he would be greater than our idea – indeed, greater than *any* ideas – existing in our minds, but it does not follow that he would be greater than what our idea is an idea of – for our idea simply is of the greatest conceivable being. So, there would be no contradiction.

Our godly dialogue, though, does not appear to involve the alleged muddle. God's argument is that if we reflect on what we mean by 'the greatest conceivable being', we should see that it involves existence. To take matters further, here comes Santa Claus.

I: But Santa Claus, you don't exist.

SC: You're right, given your understanding of 'Santa Claus'. But consider, instead, a Santa Claus with maximal generosity, most perfect white beard, best possible 'ho, ho' – and so on.

I: I'm trying.

SC: Call him, 'the greatest conceivable Santa Claus'. Then, were he not to exist, we should be able to conceive of a greater Santa Claus, namely one that exists, and so …

I: Go on, tell me – 'and so therefore the greatest conceivable Santa Claus exists.'

SC: By Santa, you've got it!

I: But then the greatest of numerous, numerous things exist – the greatest cat, dog, and pigeon; the greatest Zilli's ice cream.

SC: The universe – 'tis great indeed.

I: So great that, if such reasoning works, there exists not merely the greatest good God, but also the greatest evil Devil.

*　　*　　*

What is meant by 'greatest'? Sometimes it is understood as perfection, sometimes as maximal independent reality. Whatever the version, it includes existence and excludes features lacking in greatness. So, the greatest conceivable Santa Claus involves a contradiction because, being Santa Claus, however great, he must still be finite, limited, in many ways – for example, he must fit regular chimneys and deliver presents to human beings. For similar reasons, we need not judge that the greatest being has perfect eyesight, Estonian language skills, and tango-dancing ability. However, in the spirit of ontological arguments, could we not argue that we at least have the idea of a great Santa Claus, great in that he possesses the feature of existing? So, were such a Claus not to exist, then we should have landed ourselves with a contradiction.

Here is one way of trying to expose the error in such arguing: Were you to describe the woman of your dreams to a dating agency, you would be unimpressed if the agency suggested someone who satisfied the descriptions you gave – the predicates listed – yet who was fictional. 'Oh, but you didn't specify that she should exist,' would not quell your 'money back' demand. Yet, had you added 'and exists' in your initial requirement, that would not have been another feature, but simply that the agency produce a woman as described by the descriptions, the predicates, first listed.

With the dating agency example in mind, let us return to God. From the idea of the greatest conceivable being, we may infer that such a being has features of being all powerful and so on. But to infer 'and exists' is simply to say that there is a being that has those features. Whether there exists such a being depends on whether any item in the world satisfies the given descriptions or predicates. And how could we find that out, save by investigating the world? This line of thinking is grounded in the slogan, 'Existence is not a predicate.'

When we investigate the world, we encounter items that only happen to exist. This book, that tree, the sun, and the moon might not have existed – well, so it seems. And it is difficult to see how putting together a set of descriptions or predicates could establish that there is a thing that merely happens to exist. Yet, as said earlier, we do conclude, by reasoning alone, that round squares cannot exist and the number nineteen must exist. These examples, though, concern *necessary* existence, what *must* be so. Perhaps the idea of the greatest conceivable being points to something that necessarily exists – to something that has an existence akin to abstract mathematical entities. We may now, of course, wonder whether we do really possess a coherent idea of the greatest being involving necessary existence.

The greatest number cannot exist. Mention a number and greater ones can always be mentioned. Perhaps the idea of the greatest conceivable being – the greatest power, the greatest love – is as incoherent as the idea of the greatest number. Further, even if we can make sense of such a being and are led to think that there *must* be one, it would seem to be an abstract entity, akin to the mathematical.

Abstract entities lack causal powers. They cannot create, love, and judge; so, the greatest conceivable being, God or Allah or Yahweh, understood in that way would lack divine features as traditionally listed. And, for that matter, even if some silver tongues could persuade us that the greatest Santa Claus and greatest ice cream *necessarily* exist, such a Santa

Claus could not deliver presents in our non-abstract, concrete world – and such an ice cream could not be licked by our non-abstract tongues, be they silver or otherwise.

27. THE GREATEST MIRACLE

17. GOD, CHOCOLATE, AND NEWCOMB: TAKE THE BOX?

24. THE UNOBTAINABLE: WHEN 'YES' MEANS 'NO'

22

VEILS OF WOE: BEATS AND PEEPING TOMS TOO

When Mandy strolls along the seashore and ruffians pepper her with pebbles, she is harmed. When Zahira crosses the park, veiled in Muslim garb, and hooligans mug her, she too is harmed. Many of us, devotees of John Stuart Mill, feel that people should be free to get on with their lives as they want, so long as they are not harming others, unless those others consent. This is Mill's Harm Principle. The ruffians and hooligans are inflicting harms without justification and without consent; they simply ought not to be doing what they do. Now for puzzling cases.

Zahira is a modest woman, committed to Islam. Unbeknownst to her, when she undresses, a peeping Tom, Tom, peeps upon her. She never knows about Tom and his peeping predilections, but is she not harmed? She loves pottering in her garden, but, when summer suns shine, she stays indoors. Mandy, her neighbour, sunbathes topless.

Zahira finds it offensive; yet is she harmed? Zahira knows that Mandy leads a sexually disreputable life, dismissive of religions, prophets, and holy scriptures. Is Zahira harmed because of what she knows goes on next door, albeit veiled by curtains?

Mandy basks under the sun, on a public beach, topless, where others too are topless. Here, she is peppered by frequent glances from men who just happen to stroll nearby; they make her uncomfortable. Is she harmed? A few fundamentalist Muslims, including Zahira, and evangelical Christians, for once all united, parade along the beach. They wave placards denouncing atheists, public nudity, and sexual immorality. More harms for Mandy? She is upset by some shouts of 'hellfire' for her friends, family, and herself. 'How could they even think such things?'

Mandy gives up on the beach; Zahira gives up on the parade. They take the train back home, acknowledging each other awkwardly. In the carriage, they are peppered by the beats of leaking MP3 players, jingles from mobile 'phones, and worse. At home, they cannot escape adjacent building works' drillings during the day. And, some nights, their very different thoughts and sleep are disrupted by car alarms and burglar alarms, all false alarms. Are they harmed?

On the next sunny afternoon, Mandy returns to her garden to sunbathe, but then feels uneasy at upsetting her Muslim neighbour. Her Muslim neighbour, now indoors, feels somewhat uneasy at her condemnation of Mandy.

Where do harms begin – and end?

Mill is often criticized for not defining 'harm', but a definition is unlikely to help: witness a problem with 'games' in Chapter 15, ... *and the living is easy*. Were an accurate definition given, then it should feature the same fuzzy uncertainties that we already find in applying 'harm'. In the end, we need to consider cases: we need to consider them ... case by case.

Zahira knows nothing of Tom's peeping. However, it is not necessary to experience harms to be harmed. People are knocked unconscious and die; they are harmed, yet unaware. True, being peeped upon is not a harm like that. Some insist that it is a harm only if discovered; but that is unconvincing. Were Zahira to find out about the peeping, she would be distressed. Why? Because of what she found out about, namely being peeped upon: were that not harmful, why would she be distressed at finding out? Zahira's interests extend beyond what she experiences. It is in her interests, given her feelings about privacy, not to be peeped upon.

A compelling and similar example concerns betrayal. If you are betrayed, you are harmed – even if the betrayal remains undiscovered and has no effect on your life's progress. We are not, of course, remotely suggesting that non-experienced harms are typically as bad as experienced ones. To be peppered by gun shot is usually radically worse than being in receipt of some peeping.

What of the distress that Zahira suffers simply in knowing of, to her mind, the unsavoury activities behind closed curtains next door? In the peeping case, although Zahira experiences no distress, she is being used by Tom for his peeping pleasure. Mandy's activities, though, do not make use of Zahira. Zahira's distress results because of her *belief* that such activities are immoral; and her belief is her responsibility. Perhaps we should, then, disregard, or at least treat lightly, harms, assuming that they should even be considered as harms, that depend upon victims holding certain moral or religious beliefs. On this view, we should treat lightly Mandy's distress at the placards – as also certain religious believers' distress at some pop operas, cartoon caricatures, and prophets' names assigned to teddy bears. However, privacy violations may then also seem to merit less concern. The possible distress at being peeped upon presumably needs victims to believe such exposure is wrong. We should remember, though, that privacy violations sport the morally disreputable feature of the victims being used by the violators for their own satisfactions, without the victims' consent. It is not at all so clear that those distressed by placards, cartoons, and teddy bears' names, are being used in some disreputable way by those who cause the distress – though, of course, sometimes that may be the intention.

As for disturbances by beat music and the like, we may be generous and agree that the racketeers – so named because of their disturbances – were not intent on deliberately irritating Mandy and Zahira. Had they been so intent, then Mandy and

Zahira would have been being used, akin to Zahira being peeped upon. Maybe the racketeers are merely living their lives as they want, just as the two women are trying to live theirs.

Mandy's lifestyle offends Zahira, but only because of Zahira's religious beliefs. Do the racketeers affect Mandy and Zahira only because of the women's beliefs? Well, no. Loud noises and even quiet repetitive noises – think of dripping taps – cause discomfort, stress, and 'on edge' feelings in some people, sometimes significantly affecting their health. These harms do not appear to be dependent on belief. But the racketeers may also feel tense, if deprived of their beats and mobile burblings; perhaps they too could suffer some physical harms, if repressing what they want to do.

'Lifestyles clash.' Is that all we can say – or are there not some relevant differences here? Suppose our starting point is people sitting on the train, travelling from A to B. Let us add some activities. Mandy reads. That usually affects no one else. She falls asleep; that usually affects no one else. Non-racketeers could listen to music turned down; that would affect no one else. Harms and disputes arise because the racket is being inflicted on unwilling others.

Perhaps the morally relevant feature here is the physical *one-way* imposition of harms, an imposition that offends the Golden Rule: do not do to others what you would not like yourself. Of course, even if that principle is accepted, it does not follow that it should take highest priority in our moral thinking. Further, it says nothing about what counts as 'doing the same'. Those who enjoy loud noise or leering at others may not mind loud noise and leers in return. True, we may avoid that objection by arguing that at the very least those who harm others probably do not want to be harmed themselves; but that returns us to our puzzlement about the nature of harms.

*   *   *

Displayed above are some factors that are relevant to the question of which harms are morally significant. Two points should be added.

The first. As Mill notes, even when some activities are harmful, they may rightly be permitted. Car driving leads to accidents; but travelling benefits are taken to outweigh those harms. The overall benefit of free expression may well outweigh the distress caused to Zahira and Mandy. We should, though, be cautious when told that because certain benefits clearly outweigh certain harms it follows that therefore some specified means to those benefits are justified. Other possible means need to be taken into account. Here is an example.

Burglary prevention is, no doubt, of overall benefit. But it follows neither that burglar prevention through inefficient noisy alarms is overall beneficial nor that there may not be better means of prevention. After all, those benefits arguably could be achieved by the fun of neon lights announcing across the property 'Help, help, I'm being burgled' or, more seriously, direct alerts to the police. We may even question the necessity of much building works' noise that distresses many people, reducing their quality of life: research could probably lead to effective silencers or quiet laser equipment. Some may immediately respond that all this would be too expensive or impractical, forgetting how over the decades authorities have made similar claims about the expense or impracticality of national health services, lead-free petrol, and banning cars from city centres – the list could go on.

The second point to note. Let us not forget courtesy, grace – fellow feeling and good will. For people to insist that they should be free to do whatever they want, by way of leaking beat music, dirty shoes on public transport seats – for bars and media organizations to promote excessive drinking and loutish culture – is to display basic discourtesies and ill will. Arguably, many individuals who do these things know no better, or – and this is a sad reflection – have nothing better to do.

Are these last points a manifestation of grey beard and age – or of some minimal sensitivity that many people quietly endorse and many others would endorse once seriously reflecting on not harming others?

25. PAST CARING?

 ### 9. THE LIFE MODEL: BEAUTY, BURGLARS, AND BEHOLDERS

30. IF THIS BE JUDGING …

23

PAINTINGS, WITHIN AND WITHOUT

Paint some doors – and for a while we are painters, but not thereby painters of pictures. The difference between painters and painters, as we may bewilderingly say, is that, in paint application, house painters typically are not aiming to represent things in their brush-strokes, colours, and textures, in contrast to painters, artists, who create paintings, destined to be hung or hidden. Let us steer towards the paintings found hanging.

Gaze at clouds, stare at winter's frosty window panes, or peer at foliage – even at the dust around us, or rather, around me. A remarkable fact – a fact worthy of remark – is that what we see is more, far more, than first meets the eye. In the clouds, the frost, the leaves – the dust – we may see a beautiful face, a grotesque beast or the smile of a friend. And when we catch that glimpse, what we see looks different from what we saw before.

The drawing here is seen by many immediately as a duck; many others see a rabbit. Most observers flick between the two, seeing the long protuberances, stretching to the right, first as a duck's beak, then as a rabbit's ears. Although the drawing may be seen as a duck – or a rabbit – we cannot see the lines simultaneously appearing as a duck and also appearing as a rabbit. That is puzzling. A duck cannot also be a rabbit, so perhaps it is impossible for something to appear as a curious creature, a duck-rabbit. But there is no obvious contradiction in a drawing appearing to someone as a duck and also appearing as a rabbit at the same time. Yet this does not happen – apparently.

Paintings often represent – picture or depict – scenes, items, and events: people, landscapes, bowls of fruit, be they real or fictional, particular or no. The *Mona Lisa* is of a particular woman. Other paintings may represent women, but none in particular. Yet others represent what do not exist: mermaids, satyrs, and fauns. One puzzle is – and let us use 'paintings' to include drawings, when speaking generally –

How do paintings picture things?

An immediate answer is 'resemblance'; but that, almost as immediately, puzzles us. Resemblance in which respects and between what? Paintings, hanging in art galleries, usually resemble each other far more than anything they represent. After all, they are mainly rectangular in shape, on canvases, their surfaces brushed with watercolours, charcoal, or paint. The pictured horse, the landscape, the face, are nothing like blobs of paint rectangularly surrounded. Does the duck/rabbit drawing really resemble a flesh-and-blood creature rather than, say, just some other drawn lines?

Perhaps this quick criticism of the 'resemblance' approach involves a gross mistake. The painting – the canvas hanging on the wall – does not resemble the horse, the landscape, the woman's face. Perhaps, though, the content of our experience, when viewing the canvas, is similar to that of our experience when looking at a real horse, the landscape, the woman. That, however, fails to explain the experience striking us so differently, depending whether we see the lines as of a duck or as of a rabbit.

Working on the resemblance approach, some suggest that

paintings simply aim to deceive; they generate the illusion of our seeing, say, a real horse, when horses are otherwise visually absent. Now, a painting – a *trompe l'œil* – can deceive us: we may be misled into thinking that peaches are present, when in fact there is only a painting carefully placed. But most paintings certainly do not deceive, even though they represent. This chapter's drawing does not mislead spectators into thinking a duck is squashed within this book. Muse upon other representations. Photographs may be black and white, yet the photographed are vibrantly coloured. Cartoons and caricatures paradoxically *mis*represent what they represent.

These implausibilities, concerning representation as mere resemblance, lead some to flip to the other extreme, understanding representation as conventional, cultural, and not objectively resembling at all. We may agree, of course, that words, typically at least, represent by conventions. The word 'duck', 'd' followed by 'u' etc., does not resemble a duck. Paintings too, it is suggested, represent because of conventions and upbringings: witness how radically different are the styles of Impressionist, ancient Egyptian, and primitive cave paintings. As children grow up, depending upon surrounding conventions, they see some painting styles as the 'right' way of representing things rather than others. That 'right way' depends on us, not on objective resemblances out there in the world.

This conventional take on representation has major problems. Conventions exist whereby graphs represent temperature changes, yet graphs are not pictures. And is it really just a matter of convention that the *Mona Lisa* represents a woman? If this were so, then, given the right circumstances, the *Mona Lisa* could have represented a horse or hamster. There is surely at least something about a painting's look, independently of conventions and culture, which sets some boundaries.

Paintings are curious objects. On the outside, so to speak, a painting is a canvas with paint. Yet we are aware of an inside: we see the horse in the painting – as we see figures in the clouds, and a duck or rabbit in this book. We are aware both of paintings as material objects and of what they represent; paintings possess both aspects, a without and a within. We are able to 'see in'. We cannot see, for example, this chapter's drawing *as* a rabbit and duck simultaneously; but, when seeing it as one of those creatures, say, as a duck, we do simultaneously see the material object, the drawn lines, and see in those lines a duck. Awareness of this twofoldness prevents us from mistaking paintings for what it is that they represent. In seeing what is present, the configured surface, we also *see in* what is absent – a duck, landscape, or face.

Artists usually paint so that viewers do see things in their paintings. Viewers may, of course, need information, sensitivity, some prompting, in order to see what artists have intended. Once they see, the visual experience differs from what it was before – just as promptings by means of a 'quack' may enable a viewer suddenly to see the duck in the duck/rabbit. We may need to look more closely or carefully to see into some paintings – to see faces and limbs, or crags and valleys.

The visual experiences of 'seeing in' differ from those when seeing items in reality or the mind's eye. Paintings, just like words, may stimulate our imagination, but imagining scenes is not, of course, the same as seeing those scenes in paintings.

On the approach outlined, paintings represent in that they offer viewers the opportunity to *see in*. True, when we look at any written sentence, in our own language, we cannot help but see beyond the shapes to the meaning, but this is not because the shapes provide visual experiences of what is meant. We could draw the word 'duck' in such a way that we see a duck in the lines drawn – showing that there certainly is some difference between visual representation and the conventional.

We still lack an account of why it is that we see one thing rather than another *in* a painting. Appeal to resemblance may return: the shapes on the canvas, as we experience them, are taken to resemble physical figures as if seen from a viewpoint in reality. Yet this is unsatisfactory, for those visual experiences depend on what we 'see in' the paintings. We risk circularity, if we explain 'seeing in' in terms of perceived resemblance in experiences, yet explain what we experience in terms of 'seeing in'. After all, the duck/rabbit drawing does look different, depending whether we see a duck or a rabbit. Why we see what we see, when we 'see in' a painting, remains puzzling. Indeed it is puzzling that in an unmoving painting we may yet see movement. 'Is it superstition to think I see the horse galloping in a picture?' asks Wittgenstein.

*   *   *

Many people may, without reflection, assume that the puzzles of representation, of 'seeing in', do not apply to abstract paintings. When we first gaze at the abstract work of, say, Mondrian, Rothko, and Pollock, we may feel that they are far, far away from the representational. Yet, even here, we see things in the paintings. With Rothko, we may see colours hovering over or behind others, whether or not the paint was applied in that order. We may see lights shining through, moods and emotions. As we learn to *see in*, what we see before us is, in a way, no longer what we formerly saw.

And if the house painter stops us and says, 'No, that wall I've just painted is not "just painted", but is my painting – can't you see what I've painted?' we may gaze into the colour and see something in the paint, and not just a wall painted.

31. DO WE MAKE THE STARS?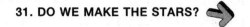

 16. 'MY BELOVED IS MINE' *or* **'THE TROUBLE WITH FOOTBALL IS THE OTHER TEAM'**

33. FRAGILE CREATURES THAT WE ARE ...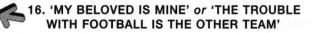

 9. THE LIFE MODEL: BEAUTY, BURGLARS, AND BEHOLDERS

24

THE UNOBTAINABLE: WHEN 'YES' MEANS 'NO'

Human that we are, we often seek the unobtainable. Jack has a great passion for Jill, but only so long as she remains aloof and unobtainable. Were she to say 'yes' to his marriage proposal, his desire would evaporate. We may sum this up by saying that Jack wants Jill if and only if she does not want Jack, that is, if and only if she does not say 'yes' to his proposal. No contradiction arises, just the misfortune of our perverse human nature.

Let us now add that Jill is a sensible and romantic woman. She will say 'yes' if and only if Jack wants her. Now, if she says 'no', then Jack wants her; so, then she should say 'yes', but that ensures that Jack does not want her – as a result, she then does not want Jack, which brings Jack back round to wanting her – and so on. The reasoning loops round and round. Let us bear this in mind, as we bring forth a little legal controversy involving Protagoras, an ancient Greek philosopher.

Protagoras gave legal training to Euathlus, an impoverished student. The condition set was that Protagoras would receive his fee, once Euathlus won his first court case. Euathlus, after his studies, gave up on the law, deciding instead to go into politics. Protagoras worried about his fee, but Euathlus pointed out that he was not required to pay until he had won a court case. So, Protagoras sued Euathlus for the fee – and lands us, seemingly, in a logical mire.

Should Protagoras get paid?

Protagoras argues that, whether he wins or loses the case, either way, Euathlus must then pay him. If he, Protagoras, wins his case for the money, then that simply means that he should be paid. If he loses the case, then Euathlus would have won his first case – and hence, by the contract's terms, he should get paid. Hence, he, Protagoras, cannot lose. Why even bother to have the case? Of course, lawyers are typically unhappy to have that last question raised.

Euathlus pursues a different line. 'If I lose the case, then I still have not won my first case, so obviously I should not pay. If, however, I win the case, then the court ruling says that I should not pay. Either way, I should not pay. Why even bother to have the case?' Of course, lawyers etc. ...

We note that Euathlus is defending himself. Were someone else defending, then they would be winning or losing. So, if Protagoras lost the case, Euathlus personally would not have won his first case – and so would not need to pay. And there would seem no grounds for Protagoras to win.

Protagoras and Euathlus present two different approaches, reaching conclusions in conflict, so something has gone wrong – but where? Perhaps the contract is itself inconsistent and hence impossible to fulfil: it seems to be saying that if Protagoras wins, then he loses, as well as allowing that if he wins then he wins – and similarly for Euathlus. Yet that criticism is itself open to criticism. The contract specifies what happens if Euathlus wins a case; it says nothing about what happens if Euathlus loses and a court rules that he should pay. We could clarify the contract by saying that Euathlus should pay Protagoras *when* and *only when* he wins a case. Let us hereafter deal with that clarified contract.

What happens if, for example, Euathlus wins the court case in which the judgement is that he should not pay? That is a contradictory situation in which, it seems, he wins and yet does not win; he should not pay, yet should pay. A similar contradiction arises if he loses the court case in which the judgement is that he should pay. The judges may anticipate the contradiction that arises whichever way they judge; they would do well to have a third way, of passing no judgement. There is, though, no reason for seeking a fence-sitting way out.

We need to attend to the saga's temporal element. Judges are being asked whether Euathlus should pay. He should not pay until he has won a case. Hence, the judges could reason that he has not won yet, until they pass judgement. Hence, they pass judgement on the basis of his not having won a case yet, and so their judgement is in his favour – and he wins. Protagoras can then take Euathlus to court again. All will then be well for Protagoras. He now successfully argues that Euathlus has indeed won a case and so needs now to pay. All would not be well if the judges had ruled that Euathlus should *never* pay; but they would have no good reason to do that.

*   *   *

The puzzle is akin to the Liar paradox. Someone sincerely announces, 'I am lying,' meaning that he is lying simply in saying that he is lying. With various caveats, if what he is saying is true, then he is not lying; but he says he is lying, so, he is telling the truth – hence, contradiction. If he is lying and so not telling the truth, then he is telling the truth because he says he is lying – contradiction again. With the Liar there is no easy temporal escape route from contradiction; this contrasts with the legal contract above. Neither truth nor falsity is fixedly obtainable in saying 'I am lying.'

Groucho Marx would not join a club that would have him as a member; and women may desire men, wanting them to propose marriage, yet once they propose, the men lose their desirability. We often want the unobtainable. The unobtainable is sometimes unobtainable because of practical matters, but sometimes because of deviancy in our wanting.

When I saw a fine burgundy velvet jacket in a sale, I

dithered: was the colour too strong, fitting too tight, price too high? When the jacket appeared to have gone, the balance was tipped: I wanted it, regretting my earlier dithering. Yet when it turned out still to be available, dithering restarted. If available, jacket not wanted; if unavailable, jacket wanted.

We often engage in activities, seeking achievements – reaching the mountain top, discovering how the story ends, satisfying yearnings of passion – yet also we resist reaching the ends, for, having achieved them, there is the anti-climax, the sadness, the emptiness. If only the bracing climb continued; if only there were another volume to the novel; if only the passion persisted … And so, in writing these words, there is the pleasure of completion, yet also some loss, some sorrow, some post-chapter'd *tristesse* – well, for the author, if not the reader.

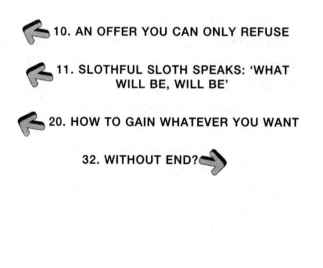

10. AN OFFER YOU CAN ONLY REFUSE

11. SLOTHFUL SLOTH SPEAKS: 'WHAT WILL BE, WILL BE'

20. HOW TO GAIN WHATEVER YOU WANT

32. WITHOUT END?

25

PAST CARING?

Allow me to make the introduction. Here is a thug, hereafter named 'Thug'. He is a complete and utter thug. Thug wallows in out-and-out violence, violence on defenceless others. He is about to be sentenced for raping, torturing, and then leaving a couple of women for dead. They survived, but have permanent injuries, both physical and psychological. He has terrorized neighbourhoods, beaten up frightened pensioners – and always with great glee. Thug stands in the dock. There is no flicker of remorse, no words of regret, no sense of guilt. Thug offers just a jeering defiant expression at the judge, jury, and victims left living.

Let us ignore practicalities of what prison sentences could or should be delivered. Let us not wonder about the best means of protecting society. Instead, let us wonder why we are, if we are, concerned about Thug, *for his sake*. After all, many would defend his human rights and be concerned for his welfare. In summary:

Why should we care about Thug?

Some immediately insist that we ought not to care; others stress our humanity, to justify our helping Thug, reforming Thug, making him see the error of his ways. We may approach the puzzle from two distinct starting points, namely, whether he is someone who cannot – or who can – help what he does. That is, whether he is not truly responsible for his actions and attitudes – or whether he is truly responsible.

First, suppose he is not responsible. He cannot help what he does; he cannot help his anti-social attitudes, his violence, his jeers. He is, in some way, victim of forces outside his control. That is possible. We recognize that brain damage, drugs, and unknown factors can cause people to act and say all manner of things. Thug, instead of acting as a free agent, is more akin to a tree being buffeted by gales, a ship broken by storms, or an insect driven by surrounding scents and colours. In this case, we may think of Thug as needing – and deserving – treatment rather than punishment, aid rather than pain.

If, indeed, he is not responsible, then he may also, though, be likened to a raging bull or a mad dog – so why not put him down? 'But that is inhumane,' it is said. 'Although he acts like an uncontrollable animal, he still possesses human rights. He has the potential to be a responsible agent, to be a person.'

But suppose that there is no cure for Thug. Suppose there is no potential. What then? Perhaps we cling to the thought that we can never be sure. Or maybe the motivation to care is irrational and in a sense mercenary. Society has supported his growing up; so, we are disinclined to give up on our investment, even though we should. Perhaps we simply cannot help but feel sorry for him; at some level, we empathize, compassion to the fore, reflecting on how dreadful it would be to find ourselves in his position.

Turning to the second approach, we suppose he is responsible for his actions. He happily embraces what he did, shows no signs of mental illness, other than his performance of the horrendous deeds. He vaunts being Thug. Why ever should we care about him in these circumstances? Two thoughts come to mind. One starts from him; one from us.

Starting from him, many religious believers insist that there exists a spark of goodness, of God, within us all – or at least a spark of divine potential. If only we could get through to Thug's spark, then he could be improved. Even if we cannot get through, he was made in God's image; that is why we should care. This approach is not exclusive to the religious. Humanists may hold a similar view, not in terms of godly sparks, but in terms of sparks of humanity. There may be the belief that, deep down within, there must be some good, or potential for good. In view of what Thug has done, though, and his continuing attitude, we may well wonder: why believe that there is any good within him at all?

Confronting the Second World War's horrors of the murder of millions – the Shoah or Holocaust – some religious believers ask, 'Where was God?' The non-religious may ask, 'Where was man?' Both questions display a startled despair – despair that some individuals lack all sparks of divinity, all sparks of humanity, when dealing with certain other individuals or groups. Their eyes are closed to the humanity of those who have the 'wrong' looks or beliefs or origins.

Sometimes concern for Thug is based on simple thoughts such as every human being is unique and valuable. But whatever is the relevance of his being unique? Each pebble is unique, but it does not follow that it merits valuing.

Starting from us – to see why we perhaps care about Thug – we may possess a horrible feeling that we could have acted as he did. We may recognize that we possess potential for injuring others, for unkindness, even outright brutality, both calculated and spontaneous. Reflect on the sheer luck, the good fortune, of our upbringing and chances in life. Could anyone, in normal circumstances, truly want to be like Thug? That simply could not be a life-choice, save by people so damaged in their upbringing or so overwhelmed by circumstances. Might we not have been so desperate, so hopeless, or so misguided, that we would have acted in the ways of Thug? Think of how violent and brutal people can so quickly become, when whipped up. Think of neighbours burning neighbours, sparked by political crises in Kenya, Rwanda, Sudan – and many places elsewhere, including Europe.

The religious speak of 'there but for the grace of God go I', and the non-religious of our sheer good fortune in not living within such fervour and ferment.

* * *

We have deliberately ignored what needs to be done to protect society; so, let us not consider punishment as justified on the basis of deterring others. That is another matter. We remain concerned about our concern for Thug for his sake. Paradoxically, sometimes concern for him, as a free agent, is the attempted justification for punishing him.

Punishment is required, it is sometimes argued, because it respects Thug as a person, someone responsible for his actions. This is a retributive approach: a vital element is that he suffers for what he has done. If he deserves anything, it is certainly not, for example, a five star hotel, by golden sands and lapping ocean, waited on hand and foot. But how do we determine what he does rightly deserve? Use of 'an eye for an eye' principle is of no help in many cases and would lead to punishments that are morally repugnant. Would any decent person really, on reflection, want to mete out to Thug what he did to others?

What we should like, I suspect, is for Thug to repent, to be genuinely sorry for what he did – and to make some amends. This is secular penance. We may even countenance the thought that his recognition and repentance could be so heartfelt that he himself ends his life. Those who baulk at inflicting pain on the guilty should note that, in wanting Thug sincerely to repent and undergo remorse, we want him to inflict pain on himself. Remorse is not enjoyable.

Suppose Thug will not repent. Imprison him, torture him, execute him – whatever we do, suppose we cannot get him to see his ways as evil. Then, we are impotent. Then, for always, Thug claims a mysterious power over us, a power that unsettles us, that shakes our humanity or our belief in humans as made in God's image. We want to nullify, cancel, neutralize that power. If only we could break down the barrier that protects him from all moral concern, from all sense of humanity. If only we could get him to be human, to say sorry and mean it. If only …

Is that why we care about Thug?

3. A PILL FOR EVERYTHING?

14. MAN OR SHEEP?

2. ON THE RUN: ALL'S FAIR WITH BEARS?

22. VEILS OF WOE: BEATS AND PEEPING TOMS TOO

26

BEAUTY AWAKE

There is more to this puzzle than meets the eye, but let us meet the eye – and then touch the more. Sleeping Beauty has a walk-on part, or, more accurately, a sleep-on part, for her role is merely to be put to sleep and then awoken in the following little game.

It is Sunday. Beauty is truthfully informed that she will shortly be popped to sleep. What then happens – and she knows this – depends on a coin's random spin. The coin is fair. If it lands heads, she will be woken, just once, at 6.00am for ten minutes, on only one of the next five days, randomly chosen; and then returned to sleep until the end of the game. If it lands tails, she will be woken at 6.00am for ten minutes, every day of the game, then popped back to sleep, each time her memory wiped each day of any previous awakenings. The game ends on Saturday, when she is woken, her memory fully restored. Before that Saturday waking, whenever she is

woken, she remembers everything about the game's set-up; but she is not told how the coin landed. Furthermore, as said, she fails to remember any previous awakenings.

So, if the coin has landed heads, then she wakes up once – obviously not remembering any prior waking. If the coin has landed tails, she wakes up five times, once each morning, but not remembering any other awakenings during the game. Speaking roughly, tails for *total* possible awakenings; *heads* for hardly any.

The puzzle is: when she wakes up during the game, what assessment should she make that the coin landed heads – or that it landed tails? This is a question of what is it rational for her to believe, given the evidence.

What should Beauty believe when she wakes up?

A few argue that it is obviously a fifty-fifty matter. When she wakes up, she has no new information, just the information given at the game's start. At the game's start, she knew that heads and tails were equally likely. She also knew that she was bound to wake up, whether heads or tails. So, now she is awake, how can she possibly conclude that tails must have been more likely? She has nothing new to go on.

Others argue that she should believe it more likely that the coin landed tails. If she bets on tails, then, over a series of such games, she is more likely to win overall than not. Suppose the game runs twelve times, one game per week: she is likely to lose the tails bet six times because there would, on average, be six awakenings resulting from heads coming up six times out of the twelve weeks. However, it is reasonable to expect her tails bet to win thirty times: on average, tails should come up for six games, and there are five awakenings for each of those six – hence thirty bets on tails when in fact it is tails. This type of consideration leads some to the conclusion that, whenever she is awake during the game, it is rational to believe it is more likely a tails awakening.

Here is a route into the puzzle. I am walking along a long bendy road, with a thousand turnings, a tree at each, but I can see only one tree at a time – mind you, I am not paying attention to them. I know that I have taken either a road (Max route) with a thousand goats, one tethered to each tree, or a similar road (Min route), but with only one goat tethered to a tree, independently of anything to do with me. The Min route is certain to have a goat at a tree, but it is a one in a thousand chance to which tree it would be tethered. In other words, Min is guaranteed to have an unlikely feature – just as a lottery may be guaranteed a winner, but it is a one in a million chance against any particular player being the winner.

My chosen road has been randomly chosen, perhaps by a fair coin's spin. I am on the road and just happen to pay attention to a tree. A goat is tethered to it. I think: although it is certain that Min has some tree with a goat, it is highly unlikely that the one I just happen by chance to look at should be that tree. With Max, it is certain that I see a goat whenever I look at a tree. Hence, I should judge that it is highly likely that I am on Max rather than Min.

Suppose, though, that my goat love is so great that whenever I pass a tree, I am bound to pay attention to it if, but only if, it has a goat tethered. Perhaps the goatish scent attracts me. Then, whichever route I walk, the first experience of tethered goat points equally to Min as to Max. Of course, if I have a second goat sighting, then that makes Max certain. If, however, I am always utterly forgetful whether I have seen a goat tethered, then I have no idea whether a sighting is a later one or a first; so, I am back to being unable rationally to judge one route as more likely.

In this traveller's tale, we have mentioned two features that may coincide: my paying attention to a tree and its having a goat. When it is just by chance that I attend, then, for all I know, I may see a goat or no goat: it could go either way. That it goes one way rather than the other is relevant evidence for me, when judging which route I probably travel. But when my attention is determined by goatish scent, then, whichever route I am on, there is no surprise in my finding a goat, when I pay attention. And so I cannot use the goatish sighting as evidence either way regarding which route.

With Beauty, when she awakes, there is no surprise at two features happening to be conjoined, such as attending to a tree and seeing a goat. It is not as if there is a coincidence between Beauty's being awake and noticing that she is awake. Whichever way the coin came down, she is guaranteed to have the experience of waking; and, with the memory loss, all awakenings seem a first awakening. So, on any game's awakening, she has no good reason to change her initial assessment; she should continue to believe that her being in the tails game is no more likely than her being in the heads game.

What of arguments that it is rational for Beauty, whenever awake in the game, to believe tails is the more likely outcome? Some present detailed probability considerations, but perhaps – note the hesitation – the puzzle shows how rational betting can separate from what it is rational to believe. Whenever Beauty is awake, she has no more reason to believe that tails came up than that heads came up. However, if she is awake because tails came up, then she has five opportunities to bet on tails and be right; but if she is awake because of heads, she has only one opportunity to bet on heads and be right. If she bets whenever awake, she should therefore bet tails. This is not because tails is more likely than heads, but because the tails outcome offers more betting opportunities than the heads outcome.

We may now reflect that if, whenever awake, she believes it is a tails game, she would have more correct beliefs over a run of games than if she believed heads. But that does not justify the claim that what is believed is more likely to be true. The evidence justifies neither the belief that it is a tails game nor the belief that it is more likely a tails game. If Beauty wanted to increase the number of times it is likely that she believes something true, and if she could, *per impossibile*, switch on beliefs at will, then she should believe she is in the tails game, but that does not mean it is rational to believe the game is more likely to be tails than heads.

* * *

Sleeping Beauty has its source in work by Arnold Zuboff, leading him – all of us, apparently – into a marvellous metaphysics, one whereby all experiences are *my* experiences, where we are all one and the same person. Before you turn to another chapter, nodding your head sadly at some philosophers' craziness, reflect on the following.

My existence, according to the usual view, required a certain spermatozoon and ovum; and their existence depended upon a sequence of a vast number of highly specific events stretching back over generations and into evolutionary mists and mysteries. A sneeze, a delayed coach, a wrong foot, so to speak, centuries ago – and my great-great-great grandparents, for example, would not have been conceived; hence

I should not have been conceived. Is it not an amazing coincidence, on the usual view, that the very specific requirements for my existence should have come about?

Of course – though paradoxically sounding – it is often highly likely that unlikely things will happen: witness the lottery example above. But, on the usual view, we have no reason to think it highly likely that the unlikely event of *my* existing would have happened. That I exist, if I am a person distinct from others, is akin to the unlikeliness, when on the Min route, of my randomly looking up and seeing a tree with a tethered goat – but where there are trillions of trees yet still only one goat. A far more reasonable hypothesis, according to Zuboff, is that my existence occurs in a Max version of a consciousness creation. Whenever any experiences come about, they are mine. Indeed, the only factor that makes an experience mine is its first-person character; and every experience has that. If this is right, then that is what we all think, being all one individual consciousness – and yet do not think, because, in some way, consciousness is segmented.

Philosophical reflections can set minds reeling. Our reeling here requires thought on unlikeliness. The one-person view is struck by the seemingly highly unlikely coincidence of the conditions required for my existence being the conditions that arose. But we may then comment on the highly unlikely coincidence of the conditions required for this book's existence being the ones that arose. Does that show that there really is only one book? The response is: of course not, unless the book were conscious. Were it conscious, then its existence would be a coincidence *for the book*. So, the one-person view hangs a lot on my existence involving a coincidence *for me*; but what is so special about the 'for me' concerning unlikeliness? Consider a lottery where it is certain that someone would win: it is still highly unlikely that the individual who won would be the winner, even if she, the winner, is unaware of having won. We may also wonder how the one-person view accommodates the fact, seemingly unlikely, that, for example, *these* experiences, when writing these words, appear to be only within the experience of Cave and not Zuboff. And so we return to the baffling question: What is this 'me'?

Yes, philosophical reflections can set minds reeling. While our existence on the usual view is vastly, vastly unlikely, it may still be more likely than the truth, or even sense, of the one-person view. We may be tempted to sigh, 'Who knows?' And here we have as much perplexity with the nature of 'who' as with that of 'knows'.

 6. 'HI, I'M SIR ISAAC NEWTON – DON'T MENTION THE APPLES'

18. THE BRAIN

28. COCKTAILS, RIVERS, AND SIR JOHN CUTLER'S STOCKINGS

3. A PILL FOR EVERYTHING?

27

THE GREATEST MIRACLE?

Water has been turned into wine – well, so some believe. The dead have been brought back to life here on Earth; someone has walked on water. Miracles, it is said, occur at Lourdes – to date, sixty-seven, according to the Catholic Church.

Many, many people have believed in miracles. Many, many people do believe. But what is a miracle? Sometimes people speak of miraculous happenings merely when very surprising and fortunate events occur. A mother who finds her child alive in an earthquake's wreckage, when hundreds are dead, may perceive the life as a miracle. She thanks God, or gods, for her child's lucky outcome, yet, were she to reflect, she should also temper her thanks with blame for the deaths of the others. Such 'miracles' though – as when difficult surgery goes well or weak candidates pass examinations – are normally accepted as in accord with the usual and natural ways of the world.

Let us focus, for the moment, on miracles as divinely

caused events. That is one feature; but some believe that everything that happens is divinely caused. So, to avoid everything being miraculous, we need to add the condition that the events differ from what usually or naturally happens. In some way, miracles interfere with the laws of nature. Water is not the sort of stuff that turns to wine; corpses, according to known natural laws, do not suddenly sit up, alive again.

Often people believe miracles occur because they already hold a religious faith which accepts miracles; and then, certain events, which would otherwise be explained naturally, are taken to be miracles, sustaining that faith. This is, to say the least, a little self-serving. The reasoning loops round.

Some people reject miracles, even the possibility of miracles, on the grounds that any events that violate what we take to be the natural laws simply show that we have failed properly to grasp what the natural laws are. The laws are more complicated than we first thought. This rejection too is self-serving, serving those sceptical of miracles, ruling miracles out virtually 'by definition', as some may seek to rule out black swans by defining swans as white.

Is it ever rational to believe in miracles?

The question is puzzling because some people are so certain that it can be rational so to believe, whereas others flatly deny miracles. The philosopher most famously associated with a 'no' to the question is the eighteenth-century philosopher

David Hume – though a certain Thomas Woolston, writing a little earlier than Hume, outspokenly attacked biblical accounts of miracles as containing absurdities and improbabilities. Woolston ended up in prison, where he died. Hume, despite being labelled 'The Great Infidel', was much luckier – and, it would seem, less inflammatory.

Let us now shelve the 'divine intervention' feature of miracles and focus on whether it is ever rational to believe that some remarkably unusual events, going against the natural laws, have occurred. For ease, hereafter we refer to such events as 'miracles', adding 'divine', when the feature of godly intervention in particular is being addressed.

Hume's position is often seen – probably mistakenly seen – as the following: while miracles are possible, it is *always* irrational to accept as reliable any reports that they have occurred. We seem to have a paradox here. Although it is recognized that a type of event is possible and can be witnessed, it is argued that it is bound to be irrational to believe any events of that type ever happened. That sounds paradoxical. After all, it is not as if we are discussing events that can only occur when human beings did not exist. There are observers of the alleged miracles.

Why may it always be irrational to believe in miracles? Well, we have considerable evidence for our beliefs that laws of nature hold. For example, none of us, despite wishes, has ever seen water turned to wine. True, many things happen to water – freezing, steaming – and theories have been developed explaining such changes. We have, though, no evidence at all to think that water can have the intoxicating transforming possibilities reported as having occurred. Indeed, it may be partly because water has not, in the experience of billions of people, ever turned to wine that we are confident that water naturally lacks such possibility. Now, what could lead us to think that a few times, centuries ago, some water was turned into wine?

Well, a few eyewitnesses reported such a change. Could their testimony, testimony passed down, make it rational for us to believe that water underwent such change? Let us assess the different evidences in play.

On the one hand we have considerable evidence in favour of water not turning to wine – from centuries of everyday uniform experience and experimentation. On the other hand, we have considerable evidence that reports of events can be misleading, either wilfully or by accident. We should, of course, apportion our belief to the evidence. Further, very high standards must be set for reports of exceptionally unusual events. Evidence against water turning to wine: exceptionally strong. Reliability of reports of events, of testimony: sometimes low. Hence, without other factors, it would appear irrational to believe in the so-called miracle – and all other so-called miracles, for similar reasons – at least when based on what people say. It is more likely that the reports are mistaken than that the exceptional events occurred.

Are things essentially different if we personally have

experiences of the seeming miracle? Again, it may be more likely that we could offer a better explanation for what we experienced than its being a miracle. The exceptional nature of the experience, if a miracle, needs to be contrasted with the well-known fact that we make mistakes, can be misled, tricked, are tempted by the extraordinary – or are just plain tired.

*   *   *

The overall conclusion is not that we should be absolutely certain that any 'miracle' reports are false, but simply that it is irrational to believe that the reported miracles happened. However, even this conclusion is too sweeping.

Hume supposes people, of different nations, reported a darkness over the planet during the first eight days of the seventeenth century. It could then be rational to believe that that highly unusual occurrence took place, given the number of reports, different sources, and so on. This shows that Hume does not argue that it is *always* irrational to believe reported unusual events have happened – 'miracles'.

Maybe Hume's position is that it is always irrational to take the further step and believe the events were divinely caused, were divine miracles. Even here, we may wonder. Suppose that the reports of the eight days of darkness also spoke of a booming voice from the skies, speaking in all languages, telling of the creation of the world, of eternal life, of its being the voice of the one true God to be worshipped ...

Well, such an extraordinary event may lead us to think that there is some conscious power present, but it would still be a big leap to conclude that therefore the power must be an eternal all-powerful deity who is all good. After all, there is still all the suffering in the world, which at least suggests that the power in question is not thereby all good – the problem of the existence of evil in the world, a problem for those who believe in God as a being who is all good and all powerful.

It is wise to be cautious of people's reports of miracles, of apparently highly exceptional events. Such caution, though, does not guarantee avoidance of error. In the eighteenth century, the King of Siam had not seen ice. He refused to believe the Dutch ambassador's reports that, during Holland's winters, water became so hard it could support the weight of elephants. Depending on what other evidence was available to him, the King, even though mistaken, may well have been rational in believing the reports false.

As well as an event's likelihood, we need to take into account reporters' motives, their position to judge, and whether similar events would be expected to occur that could be checked. In principle, more and more evidence could be given to the King, showing that, in certain circumstances, water regularly turns to ice.

Hume nicely quipped that religious believers must be conscious of a continual miracle in their person in holding their religious belief. Perhaps that is the greatest miracle. But, of course, religious faith and belief in miracles are very common

– so, really, their existence is no miracle at all. Despite the belief's irrationality, it is far from a miracle that people believe in miracles. Indeed, it may be the very irrationality that explains why it is that so many people do believe. And irrationality is no miracle at all. After all, many believers accept that rationality alone cannot lead them to God; rather, they commit themselves to leaps of faith, or, as quipped before, hops, skips or jumps of faith.

 13. HUMPTY DUMPTY ADVISES MS TURKEY

 21. 'I AM THE GREATEST' *or* 'THERE AIN'T NO SANITY CLAUS'

 24. THE UNOBTAINABLE: WHEN 'YES' MEANS 'NO'

28

COCKTAILS, RIVERS, AND SIR JOHN CUTLER'S STOCKINGS

A cocktail unshaken or unstirred can quickly cease to be a cocktail, for the ingredients separate. When wanting a gin and tonic, your want may not be divisible, such that you want a gin, whatever the outcome regarding the tonic, or vice versa. A gin and tonic needs to be mixed – and it is the mixture you want. These simple examples remind us that some items are what they are and remain the same only if they have parts with some swirl, some mixing of ingredients. Even if the parts remain constant, the items may not – and that can be simply because of absence of swirl, absence of mixing.

The cocktail ceased to be; yet the ingredients remained. Rivers remain; yet the ingredients change. An oft-cited remark in connection with this is from the early fifth-century BC ancient Greek philosopher, Heraclitus:

You cannot step into the same river twice.

Quick-fired responses have been that you cannot even step into the same river once. They may depend on a logical point that stepping into *the same* implies stepping more than once. They may, though, be relying on the fact that the waters are forever changing, whether you step once or twice.

What may have intrigued Heraclitus – and what has intrigued later philosophers – is that when Heraclitus first bathed in the river, he was indeed bathing in some water. The river consisted of just that water and nothing else. Yet the next time when he bathed in the same river, because the waters had flowed, he bathed in some different water, even though the river was the same river.

How can the river be the same, yet the water be different?

The river is, of course, extended in space; so, at one and the same time, two different people may be bathing in the same river yet in different patches of water, just as two people may be seeing the same mountain, yet one sees its bare rock to the south and the other its forests to the north. Some would then urge that the river be thought of as stretched not merely in space but also in time, as having not merely spatial but also temporal parts. We may then account for how bathing at the same location, in the same river, but at different times, may involve bathing in different waters.

Strictly speaking – a dangerous expression – Heraclitus

bathed in one temporal slice of river, identical with a patch of water, at one moment on one day; he then bathed in a distinct temporal slice of the river, identical with a different patch of water, at a later time. The first temporal slice is not identical with the second, but both are slices of the one temporally extended river.

Thinking of items, such as rivers, pokers, and people, as collections of temporal slices, though, seems to lose the idea that one and the same thing endures yet changes – a problem outlined in Chapter 4, *In no time at all*.

A more obvious response to the Heraclitean aphorism is to resist the identity of the river with its waters, making instead the common-sense observation that a river is *composed* of water. One and the same river is composed of ever-changing waters – otherwise it would not be a river, but perhaps a long thin lake. What makes something one and the same river does not depend on its possessing the same composition, the same watery ingredients, over time – and, with cocktails in mind, even when something has the same ingredients, it does not follow that it is the same item. Heraclitus, in his thinking, may have simply been making, albeit enigmatically, that common-sense point. Indeed, he offers a cocktail example: 'The barley drink disintegrates if it is not stirred.'

Changes in composition can be essential to the identity of a thing. That the river yesterday is the same river as the one today does not amount to its having the same composition. But then, what does make it the same river?

*   *   *

Sir John Cutler, of the seventeenth century, was much attached to his black worsted stockings, so attached that, as holes developed, his maid would darn them, with silken thread. Eventually, his stockings no longer consisted of the original material, but of silk. The composition of his stockings was clearly different. Yet, it could reasonably be said, they remained the same stockings, in that they possessed a continuity through space and time and were used by Sir John to cover his legs to fine effect. What made them the same stockings did not depend on material sameness, but on continuity, ownership, and function.

And what makes something the same river depends on location, usually a long geographical continuity, and changing waters flowing into a sea. A river may be the same river over time, even if during a period it runs dry, but is later replenished. And there will be times when we are unsure what to say, when rivers flow into each other. It may seem not to matter until, so to speak, it matters – as when there may be disputes about land or irrigation or fishing rights.

Here is a much discussed further example. As the parts of the Duke of Theseus's ship wore out, they were replaced, plank by plank, sail by sail, rope by rope, until – as with Sir John's stockings – not one of the original parts remained in the ship. The tale of Theseus's ship, though, has a twist. Suppose scavengers hoarded all the worn-out planks and other parts cast asunder, and then reconstructed the original ship, admittedly excessively shabby and unseaworthy. Which is really Theseus's ship – the one now composed of new parts, yet in Theseus's continual ownership, or the shabby one consisting of the original materials?

We may again be tempted by the thought that there is no 'really' about it, just a matter of decision. Here, though, it is a decision with consequences – especially if Theseus's new-looking ship is lost at sea, yet insurance companies refuse to pay out, claiming that the ship insured was the one composed of the same material, not the one now lost.

Identity itself can make us feel bewildered, at sea, especially when we raise the question of the identity of ourselves. It is all very well speaking of its just being a matter of stipulation, of decision, of words, which ship counts as Theseus's, or when a river counts as the same river; but when we think of a person continuing over time, yet also changing, whatever makes her or him the same person? Now, that does matter.

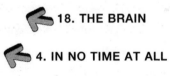

18. THE BRAIN

4. IN NO TIME AT ALL

8. WHEN ONE MAKES TWO: DRESSING UP

31. DO WE MAKE THE STARS?

29

HOVE AND LATE: A GRUESOME AFFAIR

Even the closest friends may possess little quirks. Although Miranda was a close friend, my girlfriend indeed, her little ways of calling blue things 'bleenly' coloured and green things 'gruely' irked me, though I tried to see them as sweet linguistic quirks rather than irks. I had no reason whatever to think things appeared differently to Miranda than to me; well, no more so than anyone else. After all, she called the sky 'bleen' and the grass 'grue'. And when she wore her aquamarine dress – was it really green or blue? – she wondered whether it was really grue or bleen.

What do I care, I mused, about her linguistic ways? Mind you, I thought it best not to discuss whether she considered this or that person was grue with envy; and, when we engaged in musical reflections, I resisted asking her whether she liked the bleens. My silence on such matters turned out to be sensible – for we were about to have enough troubles.

Ah, yes, there was one other little quirk. Whenever we were in romantic mood and I was declaring how much I loved her, she expressed her love too – save she said how much she hoved me. And curiously, when she expressed dislike of abstract art, football crowds, and champagne breakfasts, she would speak of lating them.

One sultry summer's day, having fallen asleep on the green grass, out in the sun, under clear blue skies, I awoke, with Miranda tugging me. She was astonished – even distressed. 'Why, what's wrong?' I asked. 'Don't you see?' she cried, 'The grass is now bleen and the sky grue – whatever am I to do?'

I was baffled. They looked the same to me. 'But, Miranda, do they look differently from how they used to appear to you?'

'Well, I suppose they must – I guess. I am not really sure what to say. The sky, though, certainly is no longer bleen; I can tell that. And I haven't suddenly changed what I mean by my words.'

I looked at the calendar: while we were asleep, there would have been a rare comet crossing the sky at the same time as a partial eclipse of the sun.

And I wondered. I wondered whatever did Miranda mean all along by 'grue' and 'bleen'? Certainly, it seemed that, after all, she failed to mean what I meant by 'green' and 'blue' – for I still used 'green' of the grass and 'blue' of the sky. But she had now switched her applications of 'grue' and 'bleen', consistently – for all blue things, she now called 'grue' and all green things she now called 'bleen'.

So, what did Miranda mean?

A quick response may be that at least Miranda must have known all along what she meant and that her meaning contained a time element. The point about time is met below. Let us recall Wittgenstein's dictum about philosophy, mentioned in the preface – 'take your time' – and so not rush in, thinking the puzzle is nonsense or easily solved. The puzzle is leading us into wondering quite what is involved in knowing what we mean.

As a small step, we need to remember that what strikes some people as 'the same' colour or shade strikes other people as different colours or shades; yet this difference may not be exposed for years – and only when the particular colour happens to be encountered by the people in question. When teaching a child how to multiply numbers, what may strike the child as going on 'in the same way' may not be what we meant by 'the same way'; and we may not discover this until much later on.

Our puzzle was made explicit by an American philosopher, Nelson Goodman, in the mid-twentieth century. It remains in the philosophical news. People, suggested Goodman, may have the colour term 'grue' and mean by it all items that are examined before a certain future time and are green; and otherwise items that are blue. In our story, we have orientated the date to an astronomical coincidence, now just past. Because we have passed that date, we can tell that something has gone awry with what we assumed Miranda meant.

On the surface it certainly looks as if, bizarrely, by 'grue' she meant what we mean by 'green' before that astronomical coincidence, otherwise what we mean by 'blue'. One unclear feature of the story is whether she experiences the grass differently. She certainly describes it with a different colour term – it is bleen, no longer grue. Another question is: given that only now have we discovered that she certainly did not mean green by 'grue', who knows her future linguistic uses?

The tale is not a play on language. Goodman initially introduced 'grue' when questioning inductive reasoning. We saw the basic induction problem in our encounter with Humpty Dumpty and Ms T, who wondered how past observations justified expectations concerning the future. There, the assumption was that at least they knew what they meant, what counted as something being the same. Goodman's 'new riddle of induction' casts that assumption into doubt.

Some reject the puzzle, arguing that the special terms are not genuine colour terms; you have to check the occurrence of the comet and eclipse – the clock, the watch, the time – before you can tell whether something is or is not coloured grue or bleen. The reply is that someone who spoke in 'grue' terms and wondered what 'green' meant could pass a similar comment. To understand use of 'green', a gruesome speaker would learn that 'green' applied to observed grue things before a certain date, or before the astronomical coincidence, otherwise to bleen things. We could resort to wavelengths, and scientific theory, in explaining our colour terms; but similar problems can arise. A Goodmanian riddle could be created by introducing bizarre terms that applied to certain wavelengths before a certain time, but to others otherwise.

The gruesome speaker projected 'grue' into the future, believing that things that were grue would remain grue; that is, according to us, would turn to blue. Why was that any more unreasonable than our projections? Did we not just have to wait and see?

*   *   *

I have presented an easy version of the riddle, but complexities have been added; the riddle has been embellished.

We had the word 'grue' to mean grue and 'bleen' to mean bleen; but suppose that Miranda – or some tribe we encounter – uses the word, the sound 'green', to mean grue, and the word, the sound 'blue', to mean bleen. We may be unable to tell that Miranda and others mean something different from us by those terms, until the key time is passed. After all, Miranda, in our original story, points to the same things as 'grue' that we call 'green'; she believes they will carry on being grue – and so on. She could do just the same, using the word 'green', but *meaning grue*. We just have to wait for her surprise when, one day, she announces that grass is no longer green, sky no longer blue. Or maybe that will be a day when *we* are surprised, suddenly thinking the sky has changed to green, the grass to blue – while Miranda insists nothing has changed, still calling sky 'blue', meaning bleen, and grass 'green', meaning grue.

We may really put the cat amongst the pigeons – poor pigeons – by asking our final gruesome question. How do we know what *we* mean when we use the word 'green'? Well, we point and say things such as, 'The colour of this grass is green – and other things are green that resemble this.' But how do we know how we shall react tomorrow, when we look at the grass? The puzzle is: what makes it the case that any one of us means one thing with a word rather than another?

Returning to our little story, I am now rightly nervous about Miranda's use of 'late' and 'hove'. Perhaps she does not mean love by 'hove', but love up to a certain date and then hate. So, in hoving me, Miranda at some future point will be hating me – yet speaking in terms of 'hoving' me still. Perhaps that is just the way that she is biologically built.

Of course, am I in any better position? How do I know what I mean, when I insist that I love Miranda and will continue to love her?

And so it is, when we say something remains the same, are we sure we mean the same when using the word 'same'?

← 13. HUMPTY DUMPTY ADVISES MS TURKEY

32. WITHOUT END? →

← 17. GOD, CHOCOLATE, AND NEWCOMB:
TAKE THE BOX?

30

IF THIS BE JUDGING ...

Lawyers and lovers, doctors and dealers, politicians and priests – all of us, in fact – face difficult and dicey dilemmas. We want to do the right thing, yet sometimes, it seems, whatever we do involves doing the wrong.

'I should be kind to people; but if I am kind to Arnold, then Zoe will be upset; and if I am kind to Zoe, then Arnold gets upset. And if I ignore both of them, they both get upset – and so do I. What am I to do?' Here, there is just one value involved – not upsetting people. Another 'one value' puzzle arises with fairness. We should be fair, so parking fines should be the same for all offenders, say £200. 'But that is so unfair. £200 is a week's wages for some, a day's salary for others. Fairness requires a percentage figure of income or capital or vehicle value.' How do we judge such matters?

Dilemmas also arise because different values, different 'right things', pull us in opposing directions. You signed a confidentiality clause about your work, yet you are now aware of some dubious dealings. Should you break your contract?

> *Terrorism*: If we torture these suspects, we may learn where the next bombings will occur; yet if we engage in torture, we're acting abominably, against our principle, our integrity. The suspects may even be innocent.

> *Love*: My future life and the life of the man whom I love would be so fulfilled if we ran away together, yet my elderly parents think it dishonourable – and I'd be letting down my husband, my commitment.

Values conflict. Absolute principles may appear fine in heavenly abstract, but, here on Earth, they engender clashes. You should never torture, yet if it is the only means of possibly saving many lives … ? How many? How strong the possibility? You should keep your marriage vows – even if your resultant years would be inauthentic? You should respect a woman's right to choose – even if you sincerely believe abortion is murder? Should governments improve the quality of lives already fortunate, through arts subsidies, rather than directing the money to ameliorate conditions for the starving?

Morality, both private and public, embraces a medley of values – freedom, happiness, promise-keeping, respect, rights, fairness, welfare – and virtues, such as courage, generosity, justice. There are also finer values: courtesy, decency, beauty, and grace. Quantities are relevant; so are qualities.

What should we do when concerns conflict – as, unnoticed, they often do; and, noticed, they sometimes do?

'It is a matter of judgement.' But while we may know what the matter is, and what the judgement eventually is, how should the judgement be reached?

How do we judge what is the right thing to do?

Sometimes judgement is easy, at least in principle. There may be a common measure between the different values, our principle being to maximize or minimize whatever is measured. We should, perhaps, maximize number of lives saved, or minimize overall suffering. Difficulties may persist. How do we assess probabilities? What is to be done, if two possible actions have equal value, with fine tuning in calculation impractical? Factual disagreements may also arise: for example, whether capital punishment deters, whether torture is effective. These are practical problems.

We focus, though, on – to my mind – a deep philosophical puzzle. What is to be done when there seems no common measure, when values turn out to be incommensurable? How can we judge between quantities and qualities concerning freedoms, rights, virtues, fairness, welfare? An action may be both manifesting someone's right to free speech, yet offending the religious. An action may be both keeping a promise, yet thereby allowing a crime to go undetected. It is not that the factors on each side of the scales are exactly balanced, but, rather – at least, it seems – we lack the scales.

This point about lacking scales requires a caveat. If the choice is between lying to a terrorist, thereby saving many lives, and telling the truth, leading to the loss of many lives, then we should lie. But when we are not at such extremes, have we any idea how to judge the right path?

Some may argue that, because we do judge in extreme cases, the scales must exist, measuring 'moral worth' or something similar, the problem being, so to speak, poor eye-sight or poor calibrations, in the difficult cases. But just because, when confronted with extremes, we often know what ought to be done, there may yet be no common measure available in the large range of less extreme cases. It is not clear how talk of 'moral worth' helps us to judge. Further, some conflicts are between, for example, items of moral worth and those of the aesthetic. Do we know how to compare the value of extending lifespans for many with saving some Venetian architectural wonders?

When facing these difficult dilemmas, we want to make wise judgements, yet the judgements may appear arbitrary or motivated by factors such as 'just how I happen to feel'. Of course, we want to distinguish our deliberations from flicks of the wrist or throws of some dice. We recognize that serious matters are involved, yet we lack, it seems, appropriate procedures for resolution.

When expert judges, in the American Supreme Court or

Britain's House of Lords, speak of weighing the evidence, balancing factors, yet reach opposite conclusions – with three judges, for example, concluding that free speech has been infringed and two judges concluding that it has not – is accepting the majority view as determining the right answer much better than spinning a coin? The allusion to the coin spin may appear all the more apt, when we remember that, had certain other expert judges been sitting or been appointed, then the overall decision could well have been different.

*   *   *

Moral dilemmas often irritate. People often want *the* answer, determining which one of various alternatives should be chosen, given the circumstances. Maybe, though, there is no right answer, in that sense. Maybe the right answer is that, whichever option is chosen, the choice will have good and bad features which are incommensurable. It is not as if – well, not obviously as if – there is some path that is the one right path, known by God, but undiscoverable by humans.

Sometimes we look back at decisions; sometimes we reflect: 'Now I see – that is what I just had to do.' This is where, upon reflection on choices previously available to us, we may feel that we could have done no other. That does not mean that physically or psychologically we could not have done otherwise, but that, to be the sort of people we are or have become, we could not have acted otherwise.

Consider: two pregnant young women, students, serious, same circumstances – each are deciding whether to have an abortion. They reach different decisions, despite being concerned by the same troubling factors concerning relationships, the significance of life, of becoming a mother, and the effect on their families, finances, and careers. In reaching their decisions, mysteriously they may have contributed to making their moral selves, to making themselves into the sort of people they are. One now sees her decision to have the child as courageous, valuing the creation of life, of nurturing the life within her. The other reflects upon her courage in having the abortion, committing, maybe, to developing a career, possibly a family much later on, and deeply feeling that having a child was not the right thing for her to do at her stage of life.

What are we to say?

Some may insist that one is right, the other is wrong; but perhaps that is a mistake. Perhaps they could both be right, even if, at the time, they were equally concerned about life, career, and future relationships – and so forth. Of course, some will then insist that there must have been a difference all along in what weight they gave to the different factors; but why insist on that? Perhaps the so-called difference that exists in their weightings is nothing more than their reaching different decisions.

I have provided an optimistic example: both women look back, feeling that they did the right thing – and did. However, we sometimes look back, reflecting on how wrong our decisions were, even on how difficult we find it to live with what we have done.

Human that we are, we have to judge what appears impossible to judge. What justifies the judgements that we make remains a mystery in deed – and not just in word. As we have seen with bears on the run, with equality between the sexes, with beats and peeping Toms, all we can do is muddle through.

Morality is indeed an extremely strange brew.

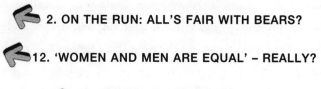

2. ON THE RUN: ALL'S FAIR WITH BEARS?

12. 'WOMEN AND MEN ARE EQUAL' – REALLY?

22. VEILS OF WOE: BEATS AND PEEPING TOMS TOO

33. FRAGILE CREATURES THAT WE ARE …

31

DO WE MAKE THE STARS?

'If the prisoners move, shoot first; ask questions later.' So came the instruction to Smart, the new guard. What a pity that Smart was a stickler for accuracy – and knew his astronomy. Later, as the other guard stared down at the dead prisoners, horrified, Smart explained that he had to obey orders and shoot. 'Don't you realize,' Smart smartly said, 'we're on Earth, so the prisoners were moving pretty fast – orbiting the sun.'

*　　　*　　　*

Whether or not something moves is relative to something else, taken as fixed, as platform. What that else is depends on context. Really, Smart was no stickler for accuracy, just obsessed with heliocentricity, with the sun as platform. Such relativity works well with motion, but surely not with the existence of objects.

Whether people are celebrities – pop stars, film stars, or just stars for being stars – depends on us; but whether stars of the sky and other heavenly bodies of non-human ilk exist is different. Of course, some things do hang on taste, are relative to taste-buds, but stars of the firmament do not. True, we may see the man in the moon – children may take the expression literally – but really there exist only configurations seen by us as fascinatingly facial. Did that face exist before humans identified it? Not at all – the face depends on our patterning inclinations; the moon and its craters do not.

Two opposed arguments lurk here:

Mind-Struck: Someone guides your eye across the night sky, pointing to constellations: there's Orion's Belt; here's the Plough – ah, Cassiopeia. Did those star patterns exist before humans existed? Certainly no one, prior to humanity, saw some stars as forming a letter W, or as being a lady with head hanging. Without such 'seeing as', would there have existed a W pattern? And the star patterns could surely have struck us as grouped differently. The groupings depend on us. There is nothing 'out there' in the night sky that brings those stars together into a W – just as there is no man in the moon.

Star-Struck: That is all very well. No doubt in some way we construct the patterns, in that the patterns we see are partially determined by what strikes us as resemblances and of interest – but those patterns are still limited by the stars and where they are. Certainly we neither made the stars nor decided where they would sparkle. We did not fix the number of planets orbiting our sun.

Mind-Struck: Until recently, that number was nine. Now, it is eight, with the sad demotion of Pluto. How many planets there are depends in part upon how we classify heavenly bodies. The planets, the stars, are but patterns of gases, chemicals, explosions, swirling molecules, and atoms. Those patterns also depend in part upon the fact that we group things in certain ways. Had we not done so, there would not have been stars ...

The general question is:

How independent of us is the universe?

It is crazy to think that the solar system – and indeed sunsets and oceans and forests and trees – were made by us. Certainly they were not physically crafted by us – and we have evidence that they existed long before we did. Surely, Star-Struck is right. And yet ...

Does not Mind-Struck have a point? Without human beings, there would have been no carving up of the world into solar systems and galaxies. It is because of our interests and the way that we perceive things that we apply terms such as 'trees', 'oceans', and 'stars'. Some differences we proclaim; others we ignore. We could have seen and carved things differently. The joints between things, so to speak, are of *our* making.

Did the wooden chess pieces, carved from a single tree, exist before we carved them? Well, no, but the tree did. Gold was not valuable until human beings bestowed value, but it existed before human beings. Did the states of the USA and countries of the European Union exist before frontiers were set and treaties ratified? True, we shaped the boundaries – but the land was there, ready to be shaped. Perhaps Mind-Struck is merely reminding us that some truths arise because of human activities, interests, and conventions; but that does not mean that all facts of the universe depend on our conventions and carvings.

And yet — that is not all that Mind-Struck is suggesting. Mention any fact and you will deploy descriptive terms; but those terms result from how we see, carve, and regard the world. The world comes to us unchopped — yet what then becomes of the world?

Look at this book. Is it one object or many? Well, it is one book, a collection of many pages, and a vast collection of electrons and other sub-atomic particles. These are different ways we have of carving the book; but is there one correct way of identifying objects, such as books, birds, and birch trees? Should we, for example, think of the tree as 'really' just a collection of cells or as one genuine unity? And the same question arises regarding the universe: is there one correct way of understanding it? Or is it undifferentiated, until we humans commence carving?

Mind-Struck is questioning whether there is just one right way of seeing things — or, at least, whether some ways get us nearer to reality than others. After all, some have seen lightning as divine thunderbolts, others as electric discharges. Surely, though, we know that one is wrong, the other right. Some say the table is solid; others say 'really' it is mainly space and sub-atomic particles. Perhaps this merely displays an ambiguity in the term 'solid'.

One approach to the quandaries is via predictions. Similarities between star patterns and shapes of the alphabet and myths concerning the gods have not generated predictions of value. Seeing books as distinct from the knees they rest upon and the hands holding them provide us with stabilities for successful predictions. We might have tried to see the hand and book as itself a unity, but that single unit so quickly and easily consists of parts, widely separated – when we move. Of course, Mind-Struck may argue that what counts even as regularities and success in prediction are also just matters of worldly carvings: we may recall Chapter 29's *Hove and late* with its gruesome affair.

*   *   *

The starting point for this puzzling picture is already a distortion. We speak of 'we' as if we are distinct from the rest of the universe. If we are, ought I not to begin the story from just me? Do I carve the universe up in such a way that I make other people?

Of course, this is crazy. I did no dividing. My awareness of the world and of myself developed within, and because of, a pre-existing community, with others using language, interacting with me. Thinking and language presuppose a world common to us all of independent perceivable objects – that is, medium-sized, reasonably stable objects. Only further investigation leads us to postulate atoms, electrons, waves, or worse. Only further reflection leads us to wonder whether the world could be seen in different ways. That does not mean that ultimately anything goes. Mind you, the question of what does – or does not – go maintains much mystery.

Let us end on a more relaxed note. Nelson Goodman tells

of someone being stopped for speeding. 'But look,' says the driver, 'relative to the car in front I was not speeding, but stationary.' The cop stamps on the road, stressing that movement relative to the road is what matters. 'But,' persists the driver, changing his tune, 'don't you know that Earth is spinning eastward; I was driving westward – so I was going even slower than those parked cars.' 'Okay,' says the cop, not to be tricked, 'you get a ticket for more or less parking on the highway – and the parked cars get a ticket for speeding.'

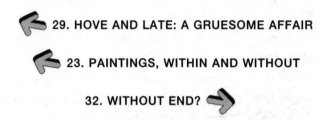

29. HOVE AND LATE: A GRUESOME AFFAIR

23. PAINTINGS, WITHIN AND WITHOUT

32. WITHOUT END?

16. 'MY BELOVED IS MINE' *or* **'THE TROUBLE WITH FOOTBALL IS THE OTHER TEAM'**

32

WITHOUT END?

Tortoises need to be taught a lesson and the lesson we have in mind for Mr T, our tortoise, is a simple piece of logic, a piece so simple that none should dispute. Here, Mr T, say we, is a valid argument, a piece of deduction upon which not even you can trip us.

'I am but a humble servant, sir, eager to learn, a devotee of that stern yet fair mistress, Miss Logic.'

'Excellent, Mr T. Let me show you the power of deduction. Suppose it true that all tortoises glory in champagne.'

'Appealing as that sounds, I fear that it is untrue, being such a humble tortoise with no pretensions to champagne and ...'

'That is why we said "suppose", Mr T, to stop you from speeding off into tales about your sorrowful upbringing with only a second-hand shell. This bit of logic is not concerned with the truth of its starting point, with its premisses, but with what can be deduced from the premisses.'

'Fair enough, sir, but please be not angry with me. I am but a humble tortoise.'

'Oh, cut that out, Mr T.'

'Right, sir, I am paying attention. I am entertaining the thought that all tortoises glory in champagne. And I bet you want me to entertain the further thought that Mr T is a tortoise.'

'That's right.'

'And you're going to tell me that, therefore, I should conclude from those two premisses that Mr T glories in champagne, even though, of course, I do not.'

'Yes. Let me set it out.

(1) All tortoises glory in champagne.

(2) Mr T is a tortoise.

(Conclusion) Mr T glories in champagne.

We know that the conclusion is false, but logic is making the point that the conclusion *follows* from the premisses (1) and (2); that is, were those premisses to be true then the conclusion would be true too.'

'That Miss Logic is very rigorous and disciplined indeed, sir. And, of course, I bow to her wisdom; but may I just check things out? For the sake of the argument – isn't that what you say, sir? – I'll accept that all tortoises glory in champagne and that Mr T is a tortoise, but – and here I must scratch both my shell and my head – I am not all that sure. Do I have to accept the conclusion that therefore Mr T glories in champagne? You see, sir, I am not sure if I quite follow – despite the sternness of Miss Logic's gaze.'

Can we help Mr T to see that the conclusion must follow?

We may be tempted to reply, with the dialogue continuing:

'Look, Mr T, can you not see, through that thick shell of yours, that ...'

'I am sorry, sir, but I have never seen through my shell.'

'It was just a manner of speech, Mr T.'

'It may be "just" to you, but not to me, brought up as I was with only a second-hand cracked shell and ...'

'Let's get on, Mr T. Can you not see that, if all tortoises glory in champagne and Mr T is a tortoise, then it must follow that he glories in champagne?'

'Ah, you mean, if premisses (1) and (2) are true, then (C) must be true ... ?'

'Exactly.'

'So, that is an important step in my grasping the argument?'

'Er, yes, I guess so.'

'We had better write it down, in case I forget it. It is another premiss that seems essential to the argument.'

'Well, yes – er, yes, yes, so the full argument is:

(1) All tortoises glory in champagne.

(2) Mr T is a tortoise.

(3) If (1) and (2) are true, then Mr T glories in champagne.

(Conclusion) Mr T glories in champagne.'

'Ah, I see.'

'I hope very much that you do see, Mr T, for if you do not, Miss Logic will grab you by your throat, dance on your shell and …'

'Now, don't get carried away, sir. Let me check it through, to make sure I understand. I accept (1) and I accept (2) and I accept (3), but, I still wonder, does (C) have to follow?'

'Oh dear, Mr T, you are a dunce. Do you really not see that if (1) and (2) and (3) are true, then the conclusion must follow?'

'I feel another premiss coming along, sir. You have just explained why the conclusion follows by giving me a premiss (4), namely,

(4) If (1) and (2) and (3), then Mr T glories in champagne.

You must pop that premiss into the argument too.'

*   *   *

At this, we all sigh, for, of course, now that Mr T has got us going, into offering additional premisses, there will be no end, well, no logical end, though there may be a weary end to the conversation. And Mr Lewis Carroll who first wrote, so splendidly, of a tortoise setting these challenges, had his Achilles writing down more and more premisses in his notebook, in his attempt to justify deduction. He would indeed need a notebook with an infinite number of spaces for writing – which, of course, all notebooks have, but that is another story about the endless division of space.

It is readily accepted that deduction cannot be justified by offering more premises. As a result, some say that what justifies particular deductions is their conforming to certain rules or schemes of logic, for example: All S are P; a is an S; therefore a is a P. I doubt if this would silence our Mr T, for, once such a rule is offered, he can set off again, asking for a further rule concerning the application of the offered rule – and so on. Further, in explaining all this, we are already making use of such deductive arguments: if you accept this Mr T, then you should accept that. You do accept this; therefore you should accept that.

*   *   *

'Er … er …'

'What is it, Mr T? About to cause more trouble for Miss Logic?'

'Certainly not. I wonder if I may help you all out.'

'Go on, Mr T.'

'Your mistake, if I may be so bold, sir, was to attempt to justify deductive practices. It was understandably kind of you to try to explain matters. Maybe making some of those comments that I forced you to write down as premises could help in some cases. Drawing little diagrams also can help. These, although valuable tricks to open eyes to validity, do not make the arguments valid. That an argument is valid, if it is, is simply manifested in, for example: (1); (2); therefore (C). Rules and schema and additional premisses do not justify (C)'s following from (1) and (2). (C) just does follow. Indeed, sir, the rules and schema are derived from the particular cases – such as the champagne case just cited.

'This too should remind some that from the premiss that a figure is a square, it validly follows that the figure has four sides. There is no need painstakingly and wrongly to insist that it only validly follows if we have another premiss such as "All squares have four sides."'

And with that, Mr T set off, his head held high – well, not that high, given his tortoise's height – muttering something about the muddles that Humpty Dumpty and Ms Turkey were getting into, thinking that inductive reasoning too needed justification. Of course, how Mr T managed to move through space and time, reaching a desired end at all, remained something of a mystery for him.

13. HUMPTY DUMPTY ADVISES MS TURKEY

15. ... AND THE LIVING IS EASY

29. HOVE AND LATE: A GRUESOME AFFAIR

21. 'I AM THE GREATEST' *or* **'THERE AIN'T NO SANITY CLAUS'**

33

FRAGILE CREATURES THAT WE ARE ...

McTaggart – John McTaggart Ellis McTaggart no less, though also no more, a philosopher at the turn of the twentieth century – kept a cat, a cat named 'Pushkin'. In winter, people who visited McTaggart in his Cambridge rooms were astonished to see Pushkin enjoying pride of position fireside front, while McTaggart shivered at his corner desk. 'Why ever do you give Pushkin the warmest slot?' 'Because,' replied McTaggart, 'that's the best it gets for a cat.'

Human beings often reflect on their lives – unlike cats. We reflect not only when in philosophy classes and on therapists' couches, but in pubs and clubs, while trapped in airports, or lazing on seashores, alone or with friends – and also in the night's stillness when sleep is elusive and only breathings and heartbeats sound. And while it is not uncommon, when the going gets tough, to wish to be feline – my mother's wish when ensnared by shrinking, twilight years – most of us value

being a person much more than being a cat. Only we humans can chart the heavens, be compassionate and just, and laugh when the barmaid, having asked which drink – 'Bitter?' she says – receives the reply, 'No, just tired.'

There is far more to human life than to the feline; and we value the more. Yet, once reflecting, we meet trouble, for we may trouble ourselves about what gives meaning or sense.

How can we make sense of our lives?

Some think that lives can only make sense if they exist for purposes beyond themselves; then, looking for purpose beyond all human lives, they are either overwhelmed with despair at its absence or embrace the mystery of purpose divine, the divine apparently requiring no purpose outside. Yet we need not quest for purposes beyond all human purposes. Making sense may occur when we cast light on moments, relationships, and activities, seeing them as holding together in recognizable patterns, with values, histories, and developments. The arts – especially the narratives of drama, novels, and opera – help us to see sense by casting light on fictional lives, that is, by telling stories.

Stories open our eyes, proposing perspectives, revealing connections, and pinpointing clashes. We may come to understand the characters' lives and meaning, through seeing how the characters connect, how their pasts stand with their futures, and which values they grow to espouse. Stories appear as myths and sagas, tales and drama, poems and opera – and today's ever-playing operas of soap. Instead of ancient gossip, Grecian in mode, about Zeus, Apollo, and Dionysus, today's lager and wine speculations anticipate the next *Sex in the City*, *Curb your Enthusiasm* or *Housewives so Desperate*.

Although the arts do not exist with the *purpose* of helping us through life, in appreciating them we may relate them to ourselves. We see how lives hang on contingencies of birth, on flicks of the hair, on chance encounters. We meet with fragilities and tragedies, yet also resolutions and magical ways of seeing. Think how, centuries on, we still live lives through Greek myths, our understanding of ourselves being shaped by updated tales and psychological theories, invoking Oedipus, Narcissus, and Helen of Troy.

A life may lack sense because experiences are fragmentary, no pattern discerned, emotions in turmoil. And, as sketched in Chapter 3's *A pill for everything?*, we may then anguish over what we truly are and want, rocked by seen and unseen conflicts. By way of example, here is a conflict, captured in Greek myth: the Apollonian versus Dionysian.

On the one hand, the image of Apollo signifies a rational world of limits, of distinct objects, of rules: a clenched fist in control. The image gives rise to aesthetic ideas of the simple, beautiful, and precise. We humans often aspire to such ideals. On the other hand, the Dionysian is intoxication, drunkenness, where boundaries become blurred, through ecstasy and frenzy: palms are open, welcoming, yielding; we melt and meld with others. Few of us think in terms of such explicit categories, itself an Apollonian enterprise; yet many of us recognize the conflict between control and succumbing – between straight lines and tangles. We need, though, the particularities of characters, details that novelists offer, that philosophy alone too easily lacks, to enlighten our struggles.

Thomas Mann's *Death in Venice*, for example, brings to life a conflict – be it through the novella, Visconti film, or Britten opera. Gustav von Aschenbach, the Apollonian personification, the disciplined writer, admirer of aesthetics, is struck by the beauty of a mysterious youth. Aschenbach's Apollonian, aesthetic appreciation transforms into a Dionysian, obsessive, sensual desire – all from afar. Aschenbach becomes desperate and degraded, degraded by an elderly man's erotic love, a yearning for youth. Yet ambiguities persist. His death on the shore, his dying gaze towards the ocean – they may generate new ways of giving sense to his life, of feeling at one.

The brief description does not captivate – but the novel, the film, the opera captivates many. We may lose ourselves in the work's beauty, while also relating to conflicts within ourselves and others. The arts, at their best, paradoxically both free us from self-absorption and shape how we see our lives and others, bringing new perspectives to bear. Religions do this too. Religious believers live lives in the light of stories, rituals, and music, derived from scriptures and tradition – though with the, arguably questionable, addition of looking beyond to an existent afterlife with God.

Let us not, by the way, foolishly and optimistically, think that good art leads to good deeds. Some tormenters – think of those responsible for the Shoah, the Holocaust – have marvelled at the splendour of, for example, Beethoven and Schubert. The arts do not make our choices for us.

*   *   *

'Life must be lived forwards, though can only be understood backwards,' wrote Søren Kierkegaard. Our life can never be grasped properly because we are never at rest to adopt the backwards-looking position. Even were we to rest, we should receive distorted pictures: how we should read the past depends in part on the future. Imagine a football game frozen ten minutes before the end: how the game is assessed up to then could differ radically from how that early period is assessed, once at end of play. What was viewed as dreadful formations, by the end is praised as inspired.

'In retrospect' has value, as does what is in prospect. Narrative art displays both: lives in prospect and retrospect. Jean-Paul Sartre saw that, prior to death, we are free to create our lives, to take them in new directions, leading to fresh 'in retrospect' views. The sting in death, according to Sartre, is awareness that, once dead, we are prey to the Other: we are impotent, as others try to interpret, fix, and classify us. Narrative art, though, should remind us that such attempts may receive continual revision. Reflect on how people debate and review interpretations of characters' lives in a play.

*   *   *

Earthly life, as also paradoxes, offers both too much and too little. There lies tragedy. Perhaps we should like all our life to be that of an itinerant global traveller, yet we may also long for a life growing within one small, stable community. We may crave the life of the unworldly, yet also the worldly; of the loyal family man, yet also the Casanova – of the woman about town, a poetess, a courtesan, yet also someone down to earth. Lifestyles rule out others. We cannot try them all. Storms rule out calm. Greyness rules out rainbows.

Many of us give wry smiles at life's clashes, incongruities, and absurdities. Pity Pushkin the cat; he knows of no absurdities, of no smiles. Yet pity us too – for we cannot know for certain how our lives finally work out. 'Pity us', did I say?

Knowledge of our lives as ultimately viewed, if viewed at all, may be knowledge best not to have; but what is worth having is the mishmash, the muddles, the mêlée of life as we live it. There is a richness to the human life that eludes Pushkin's. Not only can we humans revel in reflections, ambiguities, and humour, flying close to the sun with loves and aspirations, but also we lose ourselves in art, in music, in wonder – in wonder at the land, the sea, the stars, at the vibrant jazz of city life, and the lingering look on a face.

With philosophy an analytical and reflective art, this book's perplexities have engaged reflection – reflection upon reflection, as does this sentence. It is, though, fitting to emphasize, here at the close, that *not* reflecting also brings value, brings meaning. There can be paradoxical delight in losing the self, in simply surrendering, as perhaps Pushkin does, to dawn, to dusk, to desires – to mosaics of colours and sounds, from scuffling leaves and storms of snow to a skylark ascending over a heath. There is charm in saying nothing, in saying nothing at all. There is charm in – experiencing.

When the mountain flowers are blooming,
Their scent carries their meaning.

APPENDIX 1
FURTHER READING

My earlier book of philosophical perplexities, *Can a Robot be Human?* – hereafter *Robot* – recommended various good introductions. There are many more, so, resisting repetition, I mainly note some of the more.

For paradoxes and enjoyment, try Robert M. Martin, *There are Two Errors in the the Title of this Book* (Peterborough, Ontario: Broadview, 2002). Raymond M. Smullyan provides magnificent and enjoyable collections of logical puzzles: google for his many works. Serious recommendations for fun that raise philosophical questions are the excellent Lewis Carroll's 1865/1872 phantasies, *Alice in Wonderland* and *Through the Looking Glass*. Yes, this is the Lewis Carroll who gave us the tortoise in this book's Chapter 32. Martin Gardner's edition explains much in his *The Annotated Alice* (New York: Norton, 2000), with original texts and Tenniel's illustrations.

For seminal philosophical texts with editors' commentary: Samuel Guttenplan *et al.*, eds, *Reading Philosophy* (Oxford: Blackwell, 2003). If commentary is undesired, then Nigel Warburton, *Philosophy: Basic Readings*, 2nd edn (London: Routledge, 2005). For an encyclopaedic dictionary, seek out Ted Honderich, ed., *The Oxford Companion to Philosophy*, 2nd edn (Oxford: OUP, 2005). For the small, try Thomas Mautner, *The Penguin Dictionary of Philosophy* (London: Penguin, 2005).

Returning to paradoxes themselves, a valuable reference work remains Michael Clark's *Paradoxes from A to Z*, 2nd edn (London: Routledge, 2007). A light and introductory topic-based survey is my *This Sentence Is False: An Introduction to Philosophical Paradoxes* (London: Continuum, forthcoming).

Recent works on serious ethical perplexities include Saul Smilansky, *Ten Moral Paradoxes* (Oxford: Blackwell, 2007) and Kwame A. Appiah, *Experiments in Ethics* (Cambridge, MA: Harvard Univ., 2008). A humanist perspective on ethics and religion, expanding on some of the thoughts here, is my *Humanism* (Oxford: Oneworld, forthcoming).

APPENDIX 2

NOTES, SOURCES, AND REFERENCES

Preface and acknowledgements

For exposure of some 'postmodernist' muddle, see Alan Sokal and Jean Bricmont, *Intellectual Impostures* (London: Profile, 1998), and Sokal's subsequent works. The quip about time appears in Samuel Beckett's *Waiting for Godot* (London: Faber, 1956).

Acknowledgements are positive and praising. Let me paradoxically acknowledge some negatives. I worked in the British Library partly to avoid everlasting (it seems) construction works' inconsiderate noise and Thames Water's clattering incompetences, despite some welcome friendliness from James Fisher and Russell Harvey. Yet, in the British Library inconsiderateness also manifests itself. The library is one of the world's major copyright libraries, yet some readers have found it impossible not to scrawl in books; and some, presumably unacquainted with tissues, are incapable of reading without loud and disagreeable sniffs, and unnecessary computer jingles. Surely, *they* should know better. Sadly, perhaps they do.

Chapter 1 On thinking too much: how not to win a princess's hand

This tale deploys Gregory Kavka's Toxin Paradox. A related puzzle is Mutually Assured Destruction (MAD): a country threatens a retaliation that it would be mad to carry out. Can it be truly threatened? See Kavka, *Moral Paradoxes of Nuclear Deterrence* (Cambridge: CUP, 1987). A deeper perplexity is in my casual allusion to spotting people's intentions via brain scans. What is the relationship between neurological causal transactions and logical reasoning (raised in Chapter 17)?

Chapter 2 On the run: all's fair with bears?

Trolley/tram scenarios, trapped miners, violinists plugged into you, people falling on others with ever-ready ray guns – such tales abound. See Jeff McMahan, *The Ethics of Killing* (New York: OUP, 2002). Some stimulating thoughts are in Helen Frowe's 'Threats, Bystanders, and Obstructors', *Proceedings of the Aristotelian Society* 108 (London: Aristotelian Soc., 2008).

Chapter 3 A pill for everything?

'Forced to be free' is from Jean-Jacques Rousseau, *The Social Contract etc.*, ed. Victor Gourevitch (Cambridge: CUP, 1997). Isaiah Berlin made famous the negative–positive distinction: see *Liberty*, ed. Henry Hardy (Oxford: OUP, 2002). Many think Berlin invented the distinction, but it goes back arguably as far as the eighteenth-century Benjamin Constant, even earlier. For interweaving concerns, see Adam Swift, *Political Philosophy* (Cambridge: Polity, 2001).

The Pill Puzzle rests on metaphysical problems of freely choosing, without a platform of wants. See Gary Watson's *Free Will*, 2nd edn (Oxford: OUP, 2003). A 'chicken and egg' worry: Louise M. Antony, ed., *Philosophers without Gods* (Oxford: OUP, 2007), reminds me of David Owens' talk containing a pill story. Mine derives, I think, from my old BBC pilot sketch and related tales played over the years. Still, Owens' excellent 'future pharmacy' is in his 'Disenchantment' in Antony's collection. Owens fights the thought that science could explain everything, undermining all values. A quick reflection is: science itself rests on a truth-seeking value.

Chapter 4 In no time at all

Time baffles. A recent work is Robin le Poidevin, *The Images of Time* (Oxford: OUP, 2007). St Augustine's bafflement is in his *Confessions*, trans. F. J. Sheed (Indianapolis: Hackett, 2006).

For a fine introduction and survey concerning the many complexities of infinite divisibility and more, see Adrian Moore, *The Infinite*, 2nd edn (London: Routledge, 2001).

Chapter 5 Man with pulley: waving or drowning?

The teeth-clenching example is from Elizabeth Anscombe: see G. E. M. Anscombe, *Intention* (Oxford: Blackwell, 1957). Anscombe was a highly eccentric philosopher – a student, friend, and translator of Wittgenstein. She gained the philosophy chair that Wittgenstein once held. In 1970–80s Cambridge, there was also Bernard Williams, the other Cambridge philosophy professor (professorships then were rare). Philosophical seminars contained some clashes of character: atheist, quick-witted, humorous, and debonair Williams and the Catholic, meditative, somewhat shabby Anscombe. Both made significant philosophical contributions.

For a sense of Anscombe's earlier lifestyle, when at Oxford, see Mary Warnock, *A Memoir* (London: Duckworth, 2000). Bernard Williams' *Descartes* (Harmondsworth: Penguin, 1978) has a discussion of willing. 'Waving or drowning' derives from the Stevie Smith poem.

Chapter 6 'Hi, I'm Sir Isaac Newton – don't mention the apples'

This tale is essentially Bernard Williams's duplicate Guy Fawkes: see *Problems of the Self* (Cambridge: CUP, 1973). See also Derek Parfit, *Reasons and Persons* (Oxford: Clarendon, 1984). John Locke, in the seventeenth century, is a key figure, with tales of a prince entering a cobbler's body, or was it a frog's? See also references for Chapter 18. Julian Mayers is to be blamed for my succumbing to the name 'Aussie' and the gravity of the tale.

Chapter 7 Should we save the jerboa?

I have spoken of 'species' loosely, as in everyday speech. Details of biological classifications, whereby, for example, there are different species of a genus and different genera of a family, are unnecessary here.

Animal defenders and 'green' conservationists may come into conflict. See John Benson, *Environmental Ethics* (London: Routledge, 2000) and Christopher Belshaw, *Environmental Philosophy* (Teddington: Acumen, 2001).

A lighter tone is set by Archy, a cockroach but one-time poet, and Mehitabel, allegedly Cleopatra reincarnated as a cat. Archy bemoans the lack of concern for his species, in Don Marquis, *The Archy and Mehitabel Omnibus* (London: Faber, 1998). Archy and we are objecting to speciesism, to discriminating against other species without good justification.

Chapter 8 When one makes two: dressing up

You may admire and loathe one and the same person – for you fail to realize he is one and the same. So, that person has both the relational properties of being loathed and not loathed by you. This 'referential opacity' occurs when psychological attitudes such as beliefs, or modal properties such as necessities, are present. Jennifer Saul, though, through tales of Clark Kent entering a booth and Superman departing, highlighted identity problems, in the absence of attitudes and modalities. See *Simple Sentences, Substitution, and Intuitions* (Oxford: Clarendon, 2007).

The difference between what is strictly said and what is conveyed was stressed by H. P. Grice via conversational implicatures; he also spoke of files or dossiers being associated with proper names. A good overall discussion is by Laurence Goldstein in R. Haller and K. Puhl, eds, *Wittgenstein and the Future of Philosophy* (Vienna: öbv & hpt, 2002).

Chapter 9 The life model: beauty, burglars, and beholders

The window cleaner is from J. L. Austin's 'Pretending' in *Philosophical Papers* (Oxford: OUP, 1970).

The traditional nude/naked distinction is in Kenneth Clark's *The Nude* (London: Murray, 1956). Many nudes have shocked conservative academies. Manet's *Olympia* was viewed as subverting the purity of Titian's *Venus*, Olympia being portrayed as sexual, available, a prostitute – a 'female gorilla' sneered some. For some shocked receptions of nudes, see T. J. Clark, *The*

Painting of Modern Life (London: Thames and Hudson, 1985): many thanks to Derek Matravers for this reference.

Elaine Scarry links aesthetics and ethics in *On Beauty and Being Just* (Princeton, NJ: Princeton Univ., 1999). Voltaire tells of how differently a toad would conceive of beauty. Archy, the cockroach, in Chapter 7's notes, offers a cockroach's view. Archy needs to be better known.

Chapter 10 An offer you can only refuse

The Placebo Paradox derives from my 'Too Self-fulfilling', *Analysis*, 61 (Oxford: Blackwell, 2001). Even when patients are told that they will receive placebos, recovery rates may still improve compared to when receiving no pills. There will, of course, be similar puzzles concerning malebos, where what is given is believed to make things worse – my pessimistic thought.

Chapter 11 Slothful Sloth speaks: 'What will be, will be'

Cicero, in *De Fato*, speaks of the Lazy Argument as from Chrysippus of Soli, a Stoic philosopher, third century BC. Chrysippus apparently defended cannibalism and incest. For accessible related discussion, orientated to Aristotle, see Richard Sorabji, *Necessity, Cause, and Blame* (London: Duckworth, 1980). Contemporary argument is in Peter van Inwagen, *An Essay on Free Will* (Oxford: OUP, 1983).

Chapter 12 'Women and men are equal' – really?

This derives from a collection, *John Stuart Mill on ...* (London: BHA, 2006) edited by me. More detail is in Cristian Ducu and Valentin Muresan, eds, *John Stuart Mill 1806–2006 International Conference* (Bucharest: Univ. of Bucharest, 2007).

Some distinguish between sex and gender, but the thinking is confused: see Jennifer Saul, 'Gender and Race', *Proceedings of the Aristotelian Society*, suppl. 80 (London: Aristotelian Soc., 2006). The Schopenhauer is from his essays (many editions). For lifespan satire and equality myths, see respectively John Kekes, *Against Liberalism* and *The Illusions of Egalitarianism* (Ithaca, NY: Cornell, 1997/2003).

Chapter 13 Humpty Dumpty advises Ms Turkey

Mention of HD's language alludes to Lewis Carroll's Humpty Dumpty (see 'Further reading'). Wearing a financial hat topped with philosophy, I once wrote to regulators and investment companies, asking why they allowed past performance figures to be published with 'the past is no guide' – or not necessarily so. Responses were typically evasive or mute.

The good egg Ardon Lyon argues that the past is necessarily a guide: if all is jumbled in the past, then that guides us to expect some future jumbles. An accessible and enjoyable approach, denying that there is a deep problem, is D. H.

Mellor's 'The Warrant of Induction', in *Matters of Metaphysics* (London: Routledge, 1991). Hume's first offering, 1739, is in *A Treatise of Human Nature* (many editions), 1.3.

I have not yet seen the question whether the future is a good guide to the past. Is it worth pondering that little conundrum?

Chapter 14 Man or sheep?

Hobbes's comment appears in *Leviathan* (many editions), I.13. I first heard 'it could be worse' from Jerry Cohen, passing it on from – who can remember? David Hume likened us to passengers on a ship in the ocean and Ronald Dworkin gave the 'hypothetical contract' jibe. For discussion, see Jean Hampton, *Political Philosophy* (Oxford: Westview, 1997). An historical approach to democracy is John Dunn's *Setting the People Free* (London: Atlantic, 2005). For discussion of how the state and religion may co-exist, see my *Humanism*.

Chapter 15 ... and the living is easy

Bernard Suits and others have sought to define 'game'. Suits also defends the grasshopper's lifestyle. See *The Grasshopper: Games, Life and Utopia* (Edinburgh: Scottish Academic, 1979). For a brief ant–grasshopper rationality tale, see Martin Hollis, *Reason in Action* (Cambridge: CUP, 1996). Wittgenstein's 'games' example occurs in *Philosophical*

Investigations, ed. G. E. M. Anscombe, 2nd edn (Oxford: Blackwell, 1958), §§66–71.

Chapter 16 'My beloved is mine' or 'The trouble with football is the other team'

I am indebted to Simon Blackburn's *Lust* (New York: OUP, 2004) for some observations.

I encountered Poppea in Handel's *Agrippina*, in English National Opera's stunningly modern production, directed by David McVicar, 2007. Lucy Crowe was an outstanding Poppea – though not overweight. The Dryden is from his translation of Lucretius; the Donne is from 'Come, Madam'. Sartre's thoughts are in *Being and Nothingness*, trans. Hazel E. Barnes (London: Methuen, 1957). For some unsavoury features of Sartre's life and relationship with Simone de Beauvoir, see Carole Seymour-Jones, *A Dangerous Liaison* (London: Century, 2008).

Welcome, gracefully written works are John Armstrong's *Conditions of Love* and *The Secret Power of Beauty* (London: Allen Lane, 2002/04). For poetic prose, with *Song of Solomon* rhythms, try Elizabeth Smart, *By Grand Central Station I Sat Down and Wept* (London: Panther, 1966). The *Song* had little original connection with Solomon: see Marcia Falk's *The Song of Songs* (San Francisco: Harper, 1990). A disturbing and awesome piece of eroticism, sexual obsession, and mystery, with Biblical source, is Richard Strauss's music drama *Salome*, directed for The Royal Opera, London, by David McVicar (2008).

With cannibalism drawing near, I note that Immanuel Kant saw carnal enjoyment as cannibalistic: woman consumed by pregnancy, man by exhaustion.

Chapter 17 God, chocolate, and Newcomb: take the box?

The puzzle, courtesy of the physicist William Newcomb, was brought to prominence by Robert Nozick in 1969. It has not left the stage. For my take, see 'Reeling and A-Reasoning', in *Philosophy*, 79 (Cambridge: CUP, 2004). Arguably, the puzzle relates to Surprise Hanging and the Prisoner's Dilemma's 'Chicken': see *Robot*, Chapters 11 and 27.

Francis Galton tested prayer's efficacy by seeing whether European royalty – at the time prayed for by most – lived the longest lives of the affluent. They didn't. Maybe the prayers were to the wrong God or gods. I came across the Galton test in Stephen R. L. Clark, *G. K. Chesterton* (London: Templeton, 2006).

Chapter 18 The brain

There have been many 'brain in vat' discussions. This one, at heart, is Arnold Zuboff's distinctive 'The Story of a Brain', in Douglas Hofstadter and Daniel Dennett, eds, *The Mind's I*

(Harmondsworth: Penguin, 1982) – an excellent collection. For recent stimulating work, wide-ranging, see J. J. Valberg, *Dream, Death, and the Self* (Princeton: Princeton Univ., 2007). Zuboff has his own – and our – special take on these matters: see Chapter 26's notes.

Chapter 19 What's wrong with eating people? or even Who's for dinner?

For history and controversies, see Daniel Cottom, *Cannibals and Philosophers* (Baltimore MD: John Hopkins, 2001). A *Twilight Zone* tale uses the *Serve Man* ambiguity, information courtesy of Hiren Desai.

Jonathan Swift's proposal is 'A Modest Proposal for Preventing the Children of Poor People in Ireland, from Being a Burden to Their Parents or Country; and for Making Them Beneficial to the Public' – found in many collections of Swift's works. Michel de Montaigne noted that the barbarity of Brazilian cannibals, who roasted captured prisoners once dead, was nothing compared to the European barbarity of roasting prisoners alive.

For objectivity in ethics, using Montaigne's cannibalism – Montaigne was no relativist – see David Wiggins, *Ethics: Twelve Lectures* (Cambridge, MA: Harvard Univ., 2006). Meat being 'another man's person' is a quip from Appiah, cited in 'Further reading'. Recently there have been cases of people wanting to be eaten alive. For the importance of Forster's 'Only connect', see my *Humanism*.

Chapter 20 How to gain whatever you want

Such logical puzzles frequently do the rounds. The examples here are versions derived from Raymond M. Smullyan, 'Self-Reference in All Its Glory', in Thomas Bolander *et al.*, eds, *Self-Reference* (Stanford: CSL, 2006). The 'yeah, yeah' riposte to Austin was by the witty influential American philosopher Sidney Morgenbesser. For more gems, find him, via Google, in Wikipedia.

Chapter 21 'I am the greatest' or 'There ain't no Sanity Claus'

For extracts from St Anselm and detailed discussions, see John Hick, ed., *The Many-Faced Argument* (London: Macmillan, 1967). Recent attempts to defend ontological arguments are by Alvin Plantinga and Daniel A. Dombrowski: try the latter's *Rethinking the Ontological Argument* (Cambridge: CUP, 2006). The quip 'There ain't no sanity claus' is from a Marx Brothers' film, *A Night at the Opera* (1935).

Chapter 22 Veils of woe: beats and peeping Toms too

The Liberty Principle – the Harm Principle – is presented in John Stuart Mill, *On Liberty and Other Writings*, ed. Stefan

Collini (Cambridge: CUP, 1989). The Golden Rule comes in different versions. It is often associated with Christianity. I give a version from Confucius's *Analects*, a few centuries before Christ.

Many of us are inclined to support free speech, including a free press. Newspapers' main headlines, though, are sometimes exaggerated, highly misleading, and even downright nasty, yet may influence thousands of readers. Unhappiness with this does not mean an advocacy of censorship, but it could lead us to reflect that maybe some proper 'right of reply' should be available, with replies receiving as much coverage as the original misleading or disreputable articles.

Chapter 23 Paintings, within and without

Richard Wollheim introduced 'seeing in' in *Painting as an Art* (London: Thames and Hudson, 1988); for critical discussion, see Jim Hopkins and Anthony Savile, eds, *Psychoanalysis, Mind, and Art: Perspectives in Richard Wollheim* (Oxford: Blackwell, 1992).

Chapter 24 The unobtainable: when 'yes' means 'no'

Protagoras, fifth century BC, Greece, was the first celebrity sophist, offering expert instruction, especially in the persuasive arts. He demanded fees, boasting that he could always make the worse argument the better. He clearly would approve of many in the legal and political worlds. Apparently he invented the porter's shoulder pad. For the Euathlus tale, see Diogenes Laertius, *The Lives of Eminent Philosophers* (London: Heinemann, 1938). For more on the Liar, see *Robot*, Chapter 31.

Chapter 25 Past caring?

For criticism of the idea that all have moral worth, see John Kekes cited in Chapter 12's notes. For a collection directed towards punishment and secular penance, see Matt Matravers, ed., *Punishment and Political Theory* (Oxford: OUP, 1999).

Chapter 26 Beauty awake

Arnold Zuboff is a deep thinker, a splendid guy, a lecturer at University College London (UCL) – and so in a sense are we all, according to the one-person view. Crazy theories are sometimes true – and sometimes not. Zuboff's work deserves to be better known, though there is little published to be known. Look for 'One Self' and 'The Perspectival Nature of Probability' in *Inquiry*, 33/43 (Elmont, NY: Routledge, 1990/2000). See also Jerry Valberg, referred to in Chapter 18's notes, regarding 'my experiences'.

Chapter 27 The greatest miracle?

In Spinoza's *Theological-Political Treatise*, ed. Jonathan Israel (Cambridge: CUP, 2007), miracles are rejected and the Bible is subjected to historical analysis; note Israel's excellent introduction. Spinoza's work was first published anonymously, in 1670. Spinoza had already undergone a bad time, having been excommunicated from the Amsterdam synagogue. The excommunication initially was good for neither his business as merchant nor his social life. He turned to lens grinding. He was, by all accounts, a fine man, fine philosopher – and fine lens grinder.

For Hume's 'Of Miracles' and supporting essay, see Robert J. Fogelin, *A Defense of Hume on Miracles* (Princeton N.J.: Princeton Univ., 2003). Many other atheistic reflections appear in Christopher Hitchens, *The Portable Atheist* (Philadelphia: Da Capo, 2007).

Chapter 28 Cocktails, rivers, and Sir John Cutler's stockings

We have only a few fragments from Heraclitus: they are in G. S. Kirk and J. E. Raven, *The Presocratic Philosophers*, (Cambridge: CUP, 1983). For full discussion, see Jonathan Barnes' *The Presocratics* (London: Routledge, 1978). For complex and detailed modern identity discussions, see David Wiggins, *Sameness and Substance Renewed* (Cambridge: CUP, 2001).

Chapter 29 Hove and late: a gruesome affair

See Nelson Goodman's *Fact, Fiction, and Forecast*, 3rd edn (Indianapolis: Bobbs-Merrill, 1973). The riddle links with a sceptical 'meaning' puzzle some find in Wittgenstein: see Saul Kripke, *Wittgenstein on Rules and Private Language* (Oxford: Blackwell, 1982). With Kripke's book, controversy raged: was Wittgenstein's concern as Kripke surmised? Thus talk developed of the Kripkenstein view.

Chapter 30 If this be judging ...

For some discussion – not easy – concerning incommensurability and ordering options in terms of 'better than', see John Broome, *Ethics out of Economics* (Cambridge: CUP, 1999).

An ironic quip, suggesting at least a common concern for efficiency, is Chesterton's, 'Whatever we may think of the merits of torturing children for pleasure, and no doubt much to be said on both sides, I am sure we all agree that it should be done with sterilized instruments', quoted in Christian Joppke and Steven Lukes, eds, *Multicultural Questions* (Oxford: OUP, 1999).

Chapter 31 Do we make the stars?

The Goodman claims and critical responses are in Peter J. McCormick, ed., *Starmaking* (Cambridge, MA: MIT, 1996).

The 'moving tales' are in Nelson Goodman and Catherine Elgin, *Reconceptions etc.* (London: Routledge, 1988). See also R. Schwartz's 'I'm going to make you a star' in Catherine Elgin, ed., *Nominalism, Constructivism, and Relativism* (New York: Garland, 1997), whence a couple of examples are garnered.

Chapter 32 Without end?

Lewis Carroll splendidly set out the puzzle in his 'What the Tortoise said to Achilles', 1895, reprinted in a special issue of *Mind* (Oxford: Blackwell, 1995). Showing valid arguments pictorially is an allusion to Venn diagrams. More on this impossible demand, relating it to Zeno's original motion paradox of Achilles trying to catch a tortoise, is in my 'With and Without End' in *Philosophical Investigations*, 30 (Oxford: Blackwell, 2007). Zeno's motion puzzle is presented in *Robot*, Chapter 5.

Chapter 33 Fragile creatures that we are ...

For the continuing relevance of the ancient world, see Simon Goldhill's *Love, Sex & Tragedy* (London: John Murray, 2004). Søren Kierkegaard on living is in *Papers and Journals*, ed. Alastair Hannay (London: Penguin, 1996). At the political level, note George Orwell's aphorism: he who controls the present controls the past.

Some claim that fictional narratives are valuable preparation for what we may one day meet. Consider the fascination of Shakespeare's *Hamlet*. 'What are the options if I were to suspect that my uncle killed my father, took his position, and married my mother?' See Steven Pinker, *How the Mind Works* (London: Allen Lane, 1997). My comments are not supporting such speculations; the speculations run the danger of identifying what we 'really' value with what gives evolutionary success. For more on these matters, see my *Humanism*.

For Tao thoughts, see Raymond M. Smullyan's excellent *The Tao is Silent* (San Francisco: Harper, 1977) – and R. H. Blyth's *Haiku* (Tokyo: Hokuseido Press, 1947–52). The two lines quoted in the chapter are from a Zen verse. Pushkin may know that one can reflect too much, lining up with Basho's verse:

How admirable,
To think not 'life is fleeting',
On seeing the lightning flash.

APPENDIX 3

PARADOXES AND PUZZLES:
A QUICK FINDER

This list sets out some main paradoxes by traditional names, when available, otherwise by topic or puzzling area. As paradoxes intermesh, I have listed them from both of my *Perplexing Philosophy Puzzles* books, **E** for this ***Eating*** book and **R** for the previous ***Robot*** book, *Can a Robot be Human?*

INDEX

References to entire chapters are in **bold**.

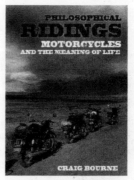